BENJAMIN
RUSH Physician, Patriot, Founding Father

SARAH R. RIEDMAN and CLARENCE C. GREEN

Physician, Founding

Illustrated with photographs

BENJAMIN RUSH

 Patriot, Father

Abelard-Schuman • *London* • *New York* • *Toronto*

LONDON	NEW YORK	TORONTO
Abelard-Schuman	Abelard-Schuman	Abelard-Schuman
Limited	Limited	Canada Limited
8 King St. WC2	6 West 57th St.	896 Queen St. W.

Printed in the United States of America
Designed by The Etheredges

TO CLARENCE GREEN

Pure scholar, rare and wonderful human being,
whose co-authorship I cherish
as the last link forged in a life-long
golden friendship chain.

His memory will always live in the minds
of the few who knew him well;
for those who may have treated him poorly,
he had not a trace of bitterness
in his heart.

Contents

Illustrations

A Note to the Reader
From One of Us

Writing "Acknowledgments" is the final loving touch the author puts on his book as it is made ready for the presses. By the finality of death, Clarence Green was denied the joy of seeing the book through this stage. A "born"-and-bred scholar with a keen sense of history, he would have been happy, as I am, to express our indebtedness first to those who restored the historical record on which rests our story of Benjamin Rush: Dr. George W. Corner and L. H. Butterfield.

With the scientific authenticity that the restorationist reconstructs the buildings of an historic period from the buried fragments of brick and mortar, laths and sills, nails and pegs, doorknocker and scraps of wallpaper, these two historiographers did the spade work, unearthing the materials needed to restore this heroic and neglected figure. Our deepest debt is to them, the first, as Editor of *The Autobiography of Benja-*

min Rush, His "Travels Through Life" together with his Commonplace Book for 1789-1813; the second, as Editor of *Letters of Benjamin Rush.* Both were published by the Princeton University Press (1948, 1952) for the American Philosophical Society. An earlier source was Nathan B. Goodman's *Benjamin Rush, Physician and Citizen, 1746-1813,* published by the same press in 1934, and based on the documents available at that time.

For background of the "portrait" — the times in which Dr. Rush lived, worked and fought — we went to many other sources: political and medical histories, biographies, the works and letters of some of Rush's great contemporaries. Each provided some precious piece to set off the man on the canvas. It was in one of many letters they exchanged, that we found the stirring words from Jefferson (to Rush): "I have sworn upon the altar of God, eternal hostility against every form of tyranny over the mind of man." They are now inscribed in the Jefferson Memorial in Washington.

For their unstinting assistance, we are grateful to the librarians and archivists in the Historical Society of Pennsylvania, Philadelphia's College of Physicians, The Ridgway Library in the Library Company of Philadelphia, The American Philosophical Society, The New York Academy of Medicine, the New York Public Library, and the Surgeon-General's Library.

Many others helped in smaller but not less meaningful ways: the person who pointed out the historic spots in the Pennsylvania Hospital, the wife of the custodian who reverently showed us through the house in Torresdale where Rush was born; the friend who thoughtfully sent us an issue of Cobbett's *Rush Light,* picked up in an old bookshop.

Finally, we are indebted to those who gave their kind permission to reproduce the photographs and engravings; these are:

Acknowledged to Dr. George W. Corner, ed. of the AUTOBIOG-
RAPHY OF BENJAMIN RUSH. HIS "TRAVELS THROUGH LIFE" TO-
GETHER WITH HIS COMMONPLACE BOOK FOR 1789-1813,
Princeton University Press, 1948
Dr. Samuel Finley
John Redman, M.D.
William Cullen, M.D.
The Royal Infirmary, Edinburgh
Melville House, Fifeshire, Scotland, Country Home of Rush's
friends, William and Jane Leslie, children of The Earl of
Levin
A street scene in Philadelphia (Third and Market Streets)

Acknowledged to College of Physicians of Philadelphia
Library and Surgeon's Hall in Philadelphia, on 5th Street be-
low Chestnut
Bookplate of Dr. Benjamin Rush
Dr. Benjamin Rush aiding sufferers in the Yellow Fever
Plague of 1793
Rush medal struck off by the U. S. Mint
Dr. Rush's Tranquilizing Chair
Statue of Benjamin Rush, Washington, D.C., maintained by
the U.S. Navy Department

By courtesy of Historical Society of Pennsylvania
Young Dr. Benjamin Rush
Benjamin Franklin
Thomas Paine
William Cobbett
Residence of Dr. Benjamin Rush, at the time of his death, 98
South 4th Street, Philadelphia

Acknowledged to The Library Company of Philadelphia
(Ridgeway Library)

A letter from Dr. Rush to a young doctor requesting information about the treatment of a patient
A letter answering an accusation "Calumnies" for Dr. Rush's part in trying to obtain a Charter for a College at Carlisle
Part of the deed of transference of property by Dr. Rush to Joseph Priestley — English chemist who escaped to America

Acknowledged to The New York Academy of Medicine
Dr. Benjamin Rush, portrait by Thomas Sully

By permission of Princeton University Press, from BENJAMIN RUSH, PHYSICIAN AND CITIZEN, 1746-1813 *by Nathan G. Goodman,* 1934
Birthplace of Benjamin Rush
Mrs. Benjamin Rush, Portrait by Thomas Sully

Facsimile, Library of Congress
The Declaration of Independence

S. R. R.

BENJAMIN RUSH
Physician, Patriot, Founding Father

1. Christ Church (Where he is buried)
2. Court House (Congress Hall)
3. State House (Independence Hall)
4. City Hall
5. American Philosophical Society
6. Library Company
7. Surgeons Hall
8. Carpenters Hall

9. RUSH lived during the latter part of his life in various houses in this neighborhood, as follows:

1791 - ca. 1794, 83 Walnut Street.

ca.1794 - 1796, 98 South Fourth Street.

1797 - 1807, S.W. corner Fourth and Walnut Streets.

1807 - 1813, 98 South Fourth Street.

10. Pennsylvania Hospital.

Map showing places familiar to Dr. Rush, in historical section of Philadelphia modified from an old map of Philadelphia

 # 1. A Conversation on Arch Street

IN EARLY FALL of the year 1775 Dr. Benjamin Rush, age 29, conducted the day's last patient to the door and bade him good evening. The doctor remained standing on the marble stoop for a moment and glanced along Philadelphia's Arch Street. He was expecting a certain Mr. Paine, but not as a patient. Dr. Benjamin Franklin, on business for the American colonies in London, had met Paine in 1774. Franklin had been struck by "those wonderful eyes of his" and had encouraged him to try his fortunes in America. He had also given Paine a letter of introduction to his son-in-law, Richard Bache, an influential merchant in Philadelphia. "An ingenious, worthy young man," Franklin had called Paine in the letter. When Paine arrived in Philadelphia in the second week of December, 1774, he was 37 years old, not so young perhaps as his great benefactor thought.

In 1766, when Benjamin Rush, the medical student, had left Philadelphia for Edinburgh to complete his studies, he himself had been armed with similar letters of introduction from some of Franklin's Philadelphia friends to their great compatriot. On arriving in London, Rush wrote to Franklin — at that time also in England on colonial business — asking him for his patronage. Franklin at once sent letters to two eminent Edinburgh physicians, Sir Alexander Dick and Dr. William Cullen. In the letter to Sir Alexander, Franklin asked him to welcome Rush as a young gentleman "with fine character, industriousness and good morals."

But having been befriended by Franklin was only one thing that Rush and Paine had in common on this fateful autumn evening in 1775. Only a few days before, they had met for the first time and had a talk in Thomas Aitkin's bookstore, where Paine served double duty as Aitkin's clerk and editor of Aitkin's *Pennsylvania Magazine or United States Monthly Museum,* a title foreshadowing coming events that the evening's talk between its editor and Dr. Rush would deeply influence. In the bookstore the two men had discovered their common interest in science and their common passionate sympathy for the poor and oppressed. They had both, indeed, already written powerful indictments of slavery. Paine's *African Slavery in America* had only recently appeared. Rush's *Address to the Inhabitants of the British Colonies* on slaveholding was three years old.

Rush made sure that his expected visitor was not in sight and then stepped back inside the house. He walked to his study, leaving its door open so that he might hear the front-door knocker. Before sitting down, he picked up from his table a small sheaf of papers and, holding them near a lighted candle, glanced through the neatly written notes for the lecture he was to give the next day as professor of chemistry at the College of Philadelphia. The candle light accentuated the large brow, the prominent, aquiline nose, and the firm mouth and chin. It was a fighter's face, the face of a man with a mind of his own. Stubborn perhaps — a little too stubborn for his medical colleagues and his Loyalist acquaintances.

He finished the notes and laid them on the table again in a neat pile. Then he took off his powdered wig, gave it a quick shake, and hung it on a wooden peg on the wall. With both hands he gave his head a brisk rub and smoothed back his hair as he went back to the table and sat down. He studied the top page of another sheaf of neatly written notes before him. As he did so, the mouth and chin seemed to grow even firmer, more stubborn. He intended to discuss these notes with Mr. Paine.

This Paine was an interesting man, he was thinking, a man after his own heart — a man of courage, a fighter, he believed. He also had a powerful pen, and a powerful pen was what Rush was looking for, what the times needed.

At this moment in 1775 Rush could not, of course, foresee how effective Paine's pen would become before another year was out, a year that was to see little but defeat and retreat for General Washington's ragged army. But Rush had read Paine's articles in the *Pennsylvania Magazine,* and being a writer himself, he knew Paine to be a writer, and a powerful one. The question was, would Paine, an Englishman who had been in America for less than a year, view the struggle with Great Britain in the same way as an American like himself?

Rush himself had had a hand in the struggle since before the onset of military action. In 1773 a letter of his to the *Pennsylvania Journal* protesting the heavy duties on British tea had helped to precipitate the Boston Tea Party. He had stood shoulder to shoulder with those who had advocated united action by the colonists in fighting the acts of repression passed by the British Parliament to avenge the Tea

Party. As one of the Philadelphia hosts of the delegates to the First Continental Congress in the summer of 1774, Rush had extended the hospitality of his home to such men as John Adams and Samuel Adams of Massachusetts, and Mr. Washington of Virginia. Another Virginia delegate, Patrick Henry, had been inoculated for smallpox by Dr. Rush.

As Rush studied the notes on his table, the events of 1775 passed before his mind's eye, and "the shot heard 'round the world" echoed in his ears once again. The date the shot was fired — April 19, 1775 — marked the beginning of war. With the battle of Bunker Hill in June, where Americans proved they could stand up against British professionals, the war had begun in earnest.

Rush frowned at the notes before him, and his eyes were troubled. His country was at war, but there was something lacking in the war, something these notes were intended to supply, and with Paine's help —

"Dr. Rush? A Mr. Paine to see you, sir."

Rush raised his eyes and saw Paine smiling over the shoulder of the housekeeper, who was standing in the doorway of the study. The doctor rose and moved toward the door. "You are welcome, sir," he said. "I expected to answer the knocker myself, but didn't hear it."

The housekeeper withdrew, and the two men shook hands. "Please take this chair by the table, Mr. Paine. We must be plain with each other, sir, and the candlelight, I trust, will help."

Paine laughed quietly and took the chair his host had indicated. Rush resumed his own chair.

"You live up to your reputation, Dr. Rush," Paine said. "I have heard that you do not mince words."

"I judge from your articles that you don't either, Mr. Paine," Rush said. "Where did you hear that about me, from my medical colleagues? They believe I go too far afield from

Young Dr. Benjamin Rush

my profession, that I meddle too much in politics." He added
wryly, "I'm afraid they don't even approve of me as a physician. We practice different systems of medicine."

Paine shook his head. "No, sir," he said, "I have heard
nothing from your colleagues. To tell the truth, I have as
little to do with doctors as my health permits."

Rush laughed. "Very sensible of you, sir."

"I mingle mainly with common folk," Paine said. "They
are my source of information."

Rush nodded. "Most of my patients are among the poor
— along the wharves and waterways, in the outlying towns."

"You have a devoted following there," Paine said.

"I sincerely hope so." Rush paused and looked at his guest
quizzically. "I should think that an educated man like yourself — "

Paine roared with amusement. "Educated! Sir, I left school
when I was thirteen to help my father, who was a poor staymaker at Thetford. I have been a common worker all my
life — staymaker, tobacconist, naval seaman, petty tax-
collector, preacher, tutor of small children, and now a clerk
in a bookstore. I can scarcely believe that I am presently also
a magazine editor and writer."

Rush was puzzled. "But I understand that when you came
to America you carried a letter of introduction from Dr.
Benjamin Franklin to his son-in-law, Richard Bache," he said.

The wonderful eyes were shining with laughter. "And you
are wondering how Dr. Franklin the American patriot came
to smooth the way in America for a British tax-collector?"

The doctor's stubborn jaw relaxed in a broad grin. "Something like that, yes," he said.

"It came about by accident," Paine said. "One day I went
to Parliament to present a petition I had written on behalf
of my fellow tax-collectors — petty excisemen. Dr. Franklin
was also there and spoke to me about it. He appears to be

as curious about petty petitioners as he is about lightning. He
is a friendly and generous man as well as a great one." He
looked with mock seriousness at his host. "I'm afraid he has
republican leanings."

"I'm afraid so," Rush said, "and I'm afraid I do, too."

"That makes three of us, then."

Rush put out his hand across the table, and Paine grasped
it warmly.

"Evidently the candlelight is having the effect I had
hoped for," Rush said. "It is helping us to be plain with each
other. You, doubtless, know that we are not alone in our
views."

Paine nodded. "I do," he said, "and especially among the
people I hobnob with. But what about the rich and the well-
born — and," he added, smiling, "the educated?"

"There," Rush granted, "we are not overburdened with
friends, though even there we have many staunch allies."

Paine leaned forward, his eyes fixed intently on Rush's.
"But allies in what cause, Dr. Rush?" he asked. "Here are the
American colonies engaged in a war with England, and yet
it isn't really regarded as a war on either side of the water.
In England it is only a naughty rebellion, and in Parliament
Edmund Burke pleads for conciliation with the rebels. Over
here there is a deal of hollering about taxation without representation, about restraints on trade, about the redress of
grievances. But I gather that most Americans continue to
think of themselves as loyal, if disgruntled, subjects of the
King, as the dutiful children of Mother England. Is this a
war we're in, sir, or a child's naughty prank?"

Rush was leaning back in his chair, his face beaming with
enjoyment. When Paine stopped speaking, his host asked
with apparent seriousness, "But think of the British Constitution, Mr. Paine, whose virtues we hear so much about these
days. Doesn't that protect us from the King's abuse?"

Paine, too absorbed in his argument to notice how much his host had been enjoying himself, exploded. "The British Constitution indeed, sir! It is the most ingenious sham ever devised by the mind of man. It is nothing but a clever device for dividing the spoils among the British owners of landed property — and among those spoils, sir, are the American colonies."

With an effort Rush managed to keep his pleasure from showing. He egged his guest on. "Are you suggesting," he asked, "that our rebellion should become a war for independence?"

Paine looked at him a moment before replying, his eyes wrinkling at the corners. "We have too much candlelight, Doctor. I am all too plain to you — as you are to me."

Rush abandoned pretense and shook with laughter. "You are right, Mr. Paine," he said, "the light makes us both plain." He held up his notes. "And what I have written here will make me even plainer, but before showing it to you, I would like to hear your reasons for thinking the colonies ought to go after their independence." He laid the notes back on the table.

"American independence," Paine said, "is a matter of simple economic expediency. The King and Parliament invariably judge matters in the light of economic advantage, so why shouldn't America? If America remains dependent she will automatically be cut off from profitable trade with England's enemies, which means most of Europe. But if America wins her independence she can trade wherever she likes — and pay no tax tribute to England for the privilege. It is ridiculous that a little tail the size of England should wag a vast continental dog. Must three million people flock to the shore every time a vessel arrives from England to find out how much — or how little — liberty the British wish them to enjoy?"

Rush seized his quill and made a rapid note of what Paine

Benjamin Franklin

had just said. "That last remark," he said, "is worth a hogshead of gunpowder. But I think your figure of speech about the tail wagging the dog could be improved in this case. This continent is more like a buffalo!"

Paine threw back his head and laughed. "You are right," he said. "A buffalo is a ponderous beast and would be mortal hard to wag."

Rush looked at him steadily. "Yes," he said, "I, too, favor independence, but at this moment there are not too many Americans who do, I'm afraid — and still fewer Englishmen like yourself."

"What was it the Virginian said in their House of Burgesses — 'If this be treason, make the most of it.' "

"Patrick Henry," Rush mused, "in a speech against the Stamp Tax." He paused a moment and then went on. "As you have suggested, the war we have been engaged in since April is confused — our ideas, our objectives are confused. Suppose we succeed in forcing a redress of present grievances, how long will it be before there will be other grievances to be redressed?"

"If I know the King and Parliament," Paine said, "it won't be long."

Rush nodded. "I believe so," he said, "and, therefore, the sooner we declare our independence, the sooner our aims will become clear. The war will then take on new vigor, for we shall be fighting *for* America, not *against* our mother country as now." He picked up the notes again and handed them across to Paine. "Here are some thoughts I have jotted down on the subject. Please glance through them."

Paine took the notes and began to read. As he did so, Rush got up and walked to a cabinet in the corner of the room. He opened the cabinet, took out a bottle and two glasses, carried them back to the table and set them down. He resumed his chair and waited for Paine to finish reading. At length Paine looked up.

"What you say here," he said, "is very much to my way of thinking. What do you propose to do with these notes?" He pushed the papers across toward Rush, who pushed them back again.

"Please keep them," Rush said. "They are the reason I asked you to come here this evening. I should like you to write a pamphlet embodying these ideas — and any others you may wish to include. The pamphlet should sharply project the idea of independence."

"Why don't you write it yourself, sir?" Paine asked. "It's your idea."

"It is yours, too," Rush said. "You had it before you came here this evening."

"That's true."

"And besides, I feel it in my bones that you have a genius for this sort of writing." He pointed to the note he had jotted down a few moments before. "This sentence about three million Americans flocking to the shore, for example. I could never have written that. I hope you will find a place for it in your pamphlet."

Paine grinned. "I haven't yet agreed to write it, Doctor."

"Yet it must be written," Rush said. "You are well read in chemistry and are familiar with the function of a ferment, a substance used to speed up a reaction."

Paine nodded. "I see what you mean," he said. "You feel that there are sentiments favoring independence that up to now have not been expressed or perhaps even realized and that a pamphlet like this might — " He groped for the right word.

"Exactly," Rush said. "It might speed up realization. It might encourage the friends of independence to stand up and be counted. Just now we don't know how many friends we have. In Philadelphia itself who can say how many, let alone in the province as a whole — or in the other provinces? And it is imperative that every friend be known, however unconscious of his true feelings he may be at this moment."

"Yes," Paine said slowly, "we need your ferment, no mistake about that."

"And I feel that I cannot supply it," Rush said, "not only because I am not a born pamphleteer, as I think you may be." He paused for a moment before going on. "I hope you will not think me merely timid when I give you a personal reason for not doing the writing myself and putting out the pamphlet under my name."

Paine shook his head. "I have heard too much to the contrary to think that," he said.

"Thank you, sir," Rush said. "You see, Philadelphia is my home. My roots are here — my family, my friends, my professorship, my practice. I have already said that my medical colleagues think me too political and that they disapprove of my system of medicine, though I learned it from one of the greatest physicians in Great Britain, Dr. William Cullen. Besides, many of my friends are hostile to a separation of our country from Great Britain. If a pamphlet of mine on this theme were to be ill-received — and I warn you that one by you might be ill-received — I shudder to think of the probable consequences. A physician cannot easily pick up and move to another community, sacrificing whatever practice and standing he may have laboriously built up."

"I understand," Paine said. "I can easily imagine how much your connections here must mean to you, not having any connections myself — here or elsewhere. I am a rolling stone, and will probably be moving on in any case." He shrugged. "If worse comes to worst, I can always fall back on tax-collecting."

"But not in England, I'm afraid," Rush said, laughing, "not after this pamphlet. You *will* write it?"

"I will."

Rush picked up the bottle he had placed on the table, pulled the cork and filled the two glasses with wine.

Thomas Paine

"You may have heard, Mr. Paine, that I am a firm advocate of temperance."

Paine chuckled as he accepted his glass. "No, that is one thing I haven't heard."

"In any case," Rush said, "I believe this is an occasion calling for a toast." He raised his glass, and Paine raised his. "To American Independence!"

"Hear, hear!"

"What will you call the pamphlet?" Rush asked. "Have you any idea?"

Paine considered. "It will contain nothing but the plain truth," he said. "Perhaps that would be a good title."

"*Plain Truth*," Rush said, trying it out. "Yes, that's good." He was silent for a moment. "But truth can be plain to some and not to others. We want a truth that is plain to everybody with common sense." He snapped his fingers. "I think we've got it. Let's call it *Common Sense.*"

"You're right," Paine said. "*Common Sense* it will be." He picked up Rush's notes, put them in his pocket and stood up.

Rush also rose and approached his guest. "Please let me see the chapters as you finish them, Mr. Paine. I have a foster father's concern."

"I will."

"And when you have completed the job, may I suggest that you show it to Dr. Franklin, James Wilson and Samuel Adams," Rush said. "I will arrange it. They are all friends of American Independence."

"Thank you, sir," Paine said. "I will do as you say."

Rush showed his guest to the door, and they shook hands. Paine started to walk away.

"Don't forget the three million people flocking to the American shore," Rush called after him.

Paine smiled back over his shoulder, raised one hand in acknowledgment and kept on walking.

 2. Christmas Eve --- 1745

IT WAS EARLY DUSK as John Rush maneuvered the light one-horse sleigh into its place under the protective roof of the lean-to on the lee side of the barn. He removed his lap robe, shook off the coating of new-fallen snow, folded the rug and stowed it under the seat. Then he took off his mittens, stuffed them into his coat pockets and climbed stiffly to the ground.

On this Christmas Eve, in 1745, John Rush was only thirty-three years old, but, after the twelve-mile drive from the farm in Byberry down along the Delaware to Philadelphia and back, he felt a lot older. For a blacksmith and gunsmith, used to moving about in his smithy, sitting still and driving in the cold was hard work.

He hurriedly unhitched the young mare, lowered the shafts to the ground and led the steaming horse to the watering trough in front of the barn. John let her take only a few

gulps and then led her into the barn. He would let the mare
drink her fill when she had cooled off and give her a good
currying and brushing before bedding her down for the
night.

He was glad now that he had put hay in the manger and
oats in the mare's oatbox before he left. James, his oldest,
was scarcely six years old, too young to pitch hay down from
the haymow, and Rachel and Rebecca were no more than babies, one four, the other two. As for his wife, Susanna —
John smiled happily as he walked out of the barn to the
sleigh, and took out some brown paper parcels, which contained the purchases he had made in the city.

His boots squeaking in the clean new snow, he walked
swiftly toward the back door of the house, sniffing the good
smell of the wood smoke he could see curling from the
chimneys at either end of the roof. Candlelight was already
brightening the windows, and through one of them he
caught a glimpse of the open iron fireplace, which people
called a Franklin stove after its ingenious inventor. He was
glad he had remembered to buy the latest edition of *Poor
Richard's Almanac.* Next to the Bible or a good sermon he
could think of nothing he liked better than Mr. Franklin's
Almanac. A sensible book that — and funny. He chuckled
at the very thought of it. After the Bible-reading tonight,
maybe he would read some of it to Susanna and the children
in front of the Franklin stove.

"I'm glad we've got a white Christmas," he thought, "for
the children's sake." Just at this moment the back door burst
open and James and Rachel came running toward him, their
faces shining with, what seemed to their father, more than
their usual welcome. Though they had run only a few yards,
they were breathless when they reached him and launched
themselves at his legs.

"He's here, father!" James cried.

Birthplace of Benjamin Rush

"An hour ago!" Rachel screeched.

The children's tackle had brought John to a halt. "You don't say," he said, looking down at them soberly. "Would you mind telling me who this remarkable gentleman is?"

James and Rachel couldn't hang on to their father's legs any longer. They were laughing too hard. Rachel fell right down in the snow and screamed, overcome by the enormity of her father's misunderstanding. James, two years older than his sister, managed to control himself and make himself understood.

"It's our brother who's here!" he cried. "Born about an hour ago! Think of it! A new brother for Christmas!"

For a moment John Rush stared down at the children, then he sprang forward toward the open door, shedding parcel after parcel as he ran. Just inside the door he pulled up. The Byberry midwife was standing before him with a howling infant in her arms. John stared at it for a moment with open mouth, then looked anxiously into the woman's eyes.

"Susanna," he said, "how's Susanna?"

"Just fine," said the midwife, "just fine. It was an easy birth."

John grinned in relief and tiptoed forward. He peered, still grinning, at his noisy offspring, then looked at the woman again.

The midwife nodded slowly.

John looked back at his son and spoke with mock sternness. "God bless you, Benjamin, I'm afraid you're going to be an orator, and I'd been planning to have you and James lend me a hand in the smithy. And now, sir, I'm going up to see your mother."

On Christmas morning John Rush drove the midwife home in the sleigh, and on the way back picked up a girl at a neighboring farm to tend Susanna. Any Byberry girl would have been glad to help the Rushes out. John, besides being the Byberry standard for honesty, was young, strong and handsome, and Susanna was a model of generosity and modesty and of housewifely prudence and piety. The neighbor girl would also help put the finishing touches on the big Christmas dinner, which probably included suckling pig, roast wild turkey, head cheese and scrapple and minor fixings — with cider to wash it all down. The table might, indeed, also have been graced with

> . . .candied apple, quince, and plum, and a heap gourd;
> With jellies soother than the creamy curd,
> And lucent syrops tinct with cinnamon;
> Manna and dates, in argosy transferr'd
> From Fez; and spiced dainties, every one,
> From silken Samarcand to cedar'd Lebanon.

No doubt the dinner was not so lavish and exotic as all this, but, as a matter of fact, some of John's purchases of the day before could have contained a few of the "spiced dainties" that Keats has Porphyro set before Madeline in his poem "The Eve of St. Agnes." The Philadelphia shops were well stocked with delicacies — some domestic, some from England, France and the West Indies, and some even from the Far East. After all, Philadelphia was the great metropolis of the colonies, and ships from all over the world tied up along her wharves.

Benjamin was not to behold the many wonders of Philadelphia for another six years, and before that he was to have two younger brothers — Jacob, later a judge of the Supreme Court of Pennsylvania, and John, who died young. His older brother, James, was named after his paternal grandfather. Benjamin's father, John, was named after Benjamin's grandfather's grandfather, the founder of the Rush family in America. In 1683, at an advanced age, this first John Rush, a rugged man, came from Oxfordshire in search of religious freedom, and settled his family on a farm in the Quaker colony of Byberry. It was a natural location, since, as Benjamin Rush in later years wrote to his old friend John Adams, the "family were a pious people and chiefly of the sects of Quakers and Baptists."

Benjamin inherited his strong religious inclinations from both sides of the family, his honesty perhaps largely, though by no means exclusively, from his father. What he certainly did not inherit from his father was the latter's meekness. Benjamin's stubbornness and fighting spirit, so clearly revealed in his features and in his career, seem to have come from the earlier John Rush, who had been a hard-riding, hard-fisted captain under his friend Oliver Cromwell in the English Civil War.

3. Philadelphia

BENJAMIN DID NOT LIVE on the farm long enough to understand the talk he later imagined as going on there — talk "about cows and calves and colts and lambs, and the comparative exploits of reapers and mowers and threshers." When he was still a small boy his father sold the house and two tracts of land at Byberry and moved to Philadelphia to make a living at his old trade of gunsmith.

The boy came to know his father only a little better than he had known the farm. John Rush died in 1751, and was buried in Christ Church Yard, when Benjamin was not quite six years old. His youngest brother, John, also died not long afterward.

The death of her husband and little boy left Susanna Rush with five children to feed and clothe and, if possible, educate. Susanna was practical and competent and lost no time in setting about her task. In October, 1751, she placed a notice in Benjamin Franklin's *The Pennsylvania Gazette*, the Philadelphia newspaper, asking the creditors of "John Rush, late of this city, Gun-smith, deceased" to come and have their accounts settled. "There is likewise to be sold," the notice continued, "A likely negroe woman, has had the small-pox and measles. Likewise a parcel of black-smiths and gun-smiths tools ... and a smith's shop to be lett."

The "likely negroe woman" to be sold may come as a shock to a reader not too familiar with the territorial extent of Negro slavery in eighteenth-century America. The plantation economy of the South made slavery more profitable there than in the North, but the fact is that there were slaves on both sides of the Potomac River, though they were much more numerous in the South. Even the best and most pious people north and south bought and sold them — people like John Rush, for example, and George Washington.

Since slaves were an expensive form of property, it was important that they be "likely" — capable, that is, and healthy. That is why Susanna Rush mentioned in her notice that her Negro woman had had smallpox and measles and was therefore now immune to them. It was particularly important that she had had smallpox, which was a wholesale killer in those days. Susanna's Negro woman is significant also because she proves that Rush's later strong abolitionist convictions stemmed from a first-hand knowledge of the evils of slavery right in his home town, not from an abstract humanitarianism. However kindly John and Susanna Rush may have treated their slave, the fact was that they were enslaving another human being and selling her when she was no longer an economic asset. This was something Benjamin would never forget.

At Byberry and later in Philadelphia, John Rush had prospered. He owned a good deal of land as well as three Philadelphia houses. But when he died, Susanna found the property not readily transmutable into gold. She had to earn a living, and chose to do so by opening a grocery and provision store. Many years later Rush wrote that "her industry and uncommon talents and address in doing business commanded success, so that she was enabled, not only to educate her children agreeably to her wishes, but to save money."

Selling groceries and provisions was about as promising a business as Susanna could have entered. A widow with small capital and five children would at least be sure that she could purchase food (and perhaps clothing as well) at wholesale prices. And Philadelphia, being the most important city in the colonies and the busiest, thronged with prosperous as well as unprosperous customers — Philadelphians, men from the ships on the river, and farmers and others from a large outlying area, for whom Philadelphia was both market and supply center.

Susanna's shop had plenty of competition from other shops that dealt mainly in staples — in flour, salt, salt fish, smoked meats, cheeses, molasses, sugar, dried fruit and preserves. Other competing shops were of the luxury type, dealing more in hard candies and spices and rum and other merchandise from the far corners of the globe.

She also competed with shops whose windows were filled with glass and china, calicoes and stays, satin breeches and silk stockings, wigs and combs, powders and perfumes and sachet bags, buttons and buckles and music boxes, lamps and candlesticks, quills and ink powder and inkwells — everything to catch the eye, and lure money from the pocketbook.

Market days were the busiest and most profitable. On these gala occasions farmers, hunters and trappers from the neighboring counties sold their produce and furs and purchased suppplies to tide them over to the next market day.

After the buying and selling and dickering were over, the outlanders were free to admire the civic genius of the efficient fire department and street-cleaning system Benjamin Franklin had devised. Some, with minds starved for knowledge, availed themselves of the educational advantages of his Library Company. All were starved for news.

Mail and news traveled at a horse's pace or at the pace of shank's mare, the legs of a man. It took three days, for example, for a mail coach to travel from Philadelphia to New York City, a distance of only ninety miles. Traveling at such a rate, news was never fresh and hardly comparable with a flash off the wires of the Associated Press. In the remoter places — such as those where some farmers and most hunters lived — there was a complete lack of news. People hungry for news had to go get it the hard way, by walking or riding or driving to Philadelphia. Here they could read the *Pennsylvania Gazette,* if they *could* read, or hear the news over a mug of ale in one of the inns and taverns.

BENJAMIN was too young perhaps when the family moved to Philadelphia to notice its strangeness, but not James and Rachel. Out at Byberry, they had never seen gentlemen in shoes with jeweled metal buckles, in silk hose and satin kne-breeches, in ruffled shirts and white cravats and in long-tailed gold-buttoned coats. James, a farm boy, was probably scornful of the young sons of these gentlemen, dressed exactly like their fathers.

These were the people who lived in the brick mansions with manicured gardens and drove glossy carriages, pulled by high-stepping horses. As Benjamin grew older, he gaped at these people and their finery with uncomfortable awe.

He was more at home among the people who lived in the little wooden or stone houses, ranged in solid rows along the narrow streets and alleys near the bank of the river. Later he

Library and Surgeon's Hall in Philadelphia, on 5th Street below Chestnut

said that he had "a natural sympathy for the poor and oppressed." Perhaps these riverside Philadelphians were not
particularly oppressed, but they were poor and had to work
hard for a living. They were the gunsmiths and blacksmiths
like his father, the small shopkeepers like his mother, the cob-
blers, wig-makers, barbers, cabinet-makers. They were the
coachmen and other out-servants of the gentlemen in satin
breeches and the ladies in gay bonnets. The working clothes
of these "little" people naturally varied with their trade or
service, but in their Sunday-go-to-meeting clothes they looked
much like the Rushes on the way to church.

As he grew older, Benjamin was allowed to join his brother
James in his exploration of the city. In their explorations,
recollections of familiar sights and sounds and smells of their
father's smithy frequently drew the boys to the blacksmith
shops. One in particular, down near the river, attracted them
like a magnet. The boys became eager, if unpaid, helpers of
the smith and took turns pumping the bellows for the forge.
When a horseshoe grew white hot in the glowing coals and
the smith plucked it out with his tongs and placed it on the
anvil, the boys would step back out of harm's way and watch
the sparks spray out from under the smith's hammer.

Watching the iron-muscled young smith was almost as
good as having their father back again. It wasn't only the
sight of the smith and his forge and anvil and hammers that
made it good. It was the sounds, too, and the smells. Especially the smells. Hot iron was one smell, and the smell of scald-
ing iron, when the smith dunked a shaped and finished shoe
in the barrel of water at his side, was another. And there
was the smell of the horse being shod and the smell of the
hoof clamped between the smith's knees when it was being
seared smooth for the fitting with a hot iron.

Nobody talked much in the shithy. But one day a few
memorable words did pass between the boys and the smith.

"You lads seem right curious about smithing," the smith suddenly said. "You aim to be smiths?"

"No, sir," Benjamin said, "I'm going to be a preacher."

"Can you talk?" the smith asked.

"He'll talk your arm off if you let him," James said.

"Not mine he won't. I won't let him." He looked soberly at Benjamin. "No money in preachin'," he said. "If you're a talker you better be a lawyer. These-here Philadelphia lawyers is the talkin'est folks I know. The best, too, they say."

 4. Golden Rule Days

BENJAMIN'S VORACIOUS READING HABITS may have been partly modeled on his father's, though John had less time than Susanna to influence the boy's education. After her husband's death in 1751, the task of educating the children was Susanna's alone, and until Benjamin was sent off to school, she was his only teacher.

Though she had attended a Philadelphia boarding school, it is difficult to say how well qualified she was for the job. We are assured by a contemporary of Susanna's that education at a girl's boarding school "was not very profound." Thus, at best, Susanna could teach her children only the rudiments of reading and writing and perhaps some simple arithmetic. The most popular reader of her time, and for a long time afterward, was the *New England Primer*, called the "Little Bible of New England." From it the children could learn the alphabet, a short list of easy syllables, and how to pronounce a few words of five and six syllables. The pronunciation list was sternly moral and included such words as *abomination, edification, humiliation, mortification,* and *purification.*

Each letter of the alphabet was illustrated by a blurred little picture and a short verse. Most of the verses dealt with biblical incidents — the "A" and "Z" verses, for example:

> In Adam's fall
> We sinnéd all.

> Zaccheus he
> Did climb a tree
> His Lord to see.

The "K" verse, however, taught love and respect for British royalty:

> King Charles the Good
> No man of blood.

Whatever Susanna was able to teach her children while they were very young, she reached the limit of her resources as they grew older and had to arrange to send them to school — at least the boys.

By 1740, Philadelphia had several private schools and private tutors — some for the rich, some for the poor — and all of them charged fees. Boys could study Latin, Greek, Hebrew, Arabic, mathematics, surveying, bookkeeping, navigation, and "natural science" of a sort. Eleven years later, inspired by Franklin, the non-sectarian Philadelphia Academy opened. It offered to teach Latin, Greek, English, French, and German as well as a large variety of practical subjects. The Academy was soon bursting at the seams, and in 1755 was reorganized as the College, Academy, and Charitable

Bookplate of Dr. Benjamin Rush

School of Philadelphia. Unfortunately, the first head of the institution frowned at what Franklin called "useful learning." Instead, he emphasized the classical learning of Greece and Rome, since Greek and Latin were thought to be in a class by themselves as mind trainers — for boys.

As a rule, even the favored young male could get a good education only in large towns like Philadelphia. Elsewhere, the schoolhouses were poor, the furnishings scant, the books few and unreadable, the teachers ignorant and tiresome, and the discipline uncommonly brutal.

One high-minded colonial poet recommended a "besomme of byrche," or broom-like switch, for beating "babes." Older culprits were beaten with a variety of simple and ingenious weapons, such as a ruler, a birch or walnut rod, a cat-o'-nine-tails, or anything that came to hand.

Fortunately, not all schoolmasters aimed to save their pupils from evil by beating virtue into them. Ministers' incomes were pretty much on a par with those of secular teachers, and most ministers eked out their salaries by taking boys into their homes to educate — humanely. The boys were then said to have been "put forth." In about 1754, when Benjamin was eight and Jacob six, Susanna put them forth with Dr. Samuel Finley, husband of her sister Sarah. Dr. Finley was a Presbyterian, who had been ordained after preaching a short time in the Second Presbyterian Church of Philadelphia. He had then become pastor of a church in the town of Rising Sun, Maryland, where he established the Nottingham Academy to train boys for the ministry.

Susanna could hardly have solved the two boys' education problem more happily. Her sister was a good-hearted, spritely woman and good for the boys' spirits. She was also a good cook and good for their stomachs. Dr. Finley—a scholarly man and later President of the College of New Jersey at Princeton — was traditionally stern, especially in the classroom, but never harsh or arbitrary. No boy could plead ignorance of a rule as an excuse for having broken it. Dr. Finley made the rules perfectly clear and definite and drove them home through repetition. When one was broken, punishment followed, but it always fitted the crime justly and was tempered with the milk of human kindness.

The stern kindliness of his Uncle Samuel and his spiritual and moral training left the pleasantest and most lasting impression on Benjamin. He never forgot Dr. Finley's solemn talks on religion or his enlightening interpretations of the Bible. A sermon was not allowed to go in one ear and out of the other. The boys had to rephrase in their own words what they had heard. In this way Benjamin began to acquire a lifelong habit of writing notes on what he had read or had heard in conversations with all sorts of people. He would then read and reread his notes to fix them in his memory.

Dr. Finley did not believe in all brains and no brawn. Play was of course one way to build the body, but work was also compulsory — as well as "pleasant and useful." On the doctor's farm the boys lent a hand with many chores and helped in the haying. "A severe cut I received in learning to reap," Rush wrote later, served, through the scar it left, to remind him of those early and happy working days.

Dr. Finley taught some science, of a kind we would not recognize today. But his main emphasis was on the "Arts" — Greek and Latin, as well as the reading and speaking of English — properly.

Grammar was important — not English grammar but Latin grammar. If you knew the latter you automatically knew the former, since it was believed that the structures of the two languages were essentially identical, a belief that persisted until relatively recent years. As Rush grew older, he came to agree with Franklin that Latin and Greek were a waste of time.

American-English spelling was not yet popularized, for it

Dr. Samuel Finley

was before the time of Noah Webster's "Blue-backed Speller" (1783). The way you spelled a word depended on how you felt. Schoolmasters, in Rush's time, presumed to teach spelling, and we may be sure that Dr. Finley was a better spelling teacher than the man in New York who advertised that he was qualified to teach "writeing and spilling."

Dr. Finley started his boys on arithmetic at about the usual age of eleven. Most teachers used a "sum book," from which they read problems to their students, mostly without explanation or even understanding on their own part. Some of the problems were monstrous. The boys were required to multiply a figure of fifteen digits by another figure of fifteen digits, to divide a figure in quintillions by a figure in billions. Sometimes these could be coped with by diligence alone, others required genius of a high order.

Finally, there was penmanship and the proper writing and folding of social and business letters. When Benjamin was at the Nottingham Academy, good penmen were very scarce. To be considered good, a teacher generally had to qualify as a good penman. Benjamin seems to have been about average in this department. At least he learned to write a legible hand.

His chief talent, as his father had jokingly prophesied at his birth, was eloquent speaking. At his age, of course, he could only be considered a good prospect for high-level declamation, but at the academy he had the good fortune to hear some expert talkers. They were not orators perhaps, these learned guests of his uncle's, but in listening to them and sometimes even conversing with them Benjamin took his first steps toward mastery of the spoken word. The distinguished visitors may not have been impressed by his budding skill, but his schoolmates were. Later on, Benjamin was most grateful of all for "the seeds of useful knowledge" these learned men planted in his mind.

Meanwhile, at thirteen, the age when he left the academy, Benjamin's mind was only a seed-bed in need of many additional seeds.

 ## 5. College and Decision

The eighteenth-century world, we are told, was one

> Where babies, much to their surprise,
> Were born astonishingly wise;
> With every Science on their lips,
> And Latin at their finger-tips

The boy who was ready might enter Harvard or Yale or Columbia at anywhere from eight to thirteen years of age, and often did, as Alexander Hamilton, for instance, at thirteen. Little girls "asked many astonishing questions about divine mysteries" and could read any book rightside up or upside down.

If we accept the precocious-child mythology at its face value, Benjamin Rush was also a prodigy. He entered the College of New Jersey at Princeton (later Princeton College, then Princeton University) when *he* was thirteen. He even outshone "that brilliant boy" Hamilton, for Benjamin entered not as a freshman but as a junior. If he had entered with his class he would have been only eleven at matriculation.

But there is an explanation for early college entrance in those days. First, there were no high schools. Boys entered college from "academies" like Dr. Finley's or from "grammar" or "Latin" schools, which were all names for the same thing. Second, college was a mere continuation of the lower schools and, except for theology and mathematics, a boy went on studying much the same things in college as he had studied in school, especially Latin and Greek. Third, there were fewer things to distract children from study than there are today, and vacations were fewer and shorter.

Benjamin's luck in being able to go to college at all is partly to be explained by his recognized ability, partly by his mother's industry and saving ways, and partly by the superior training he received at the Nottingham Academy. Full realization came only at college, where he learned that Dr. Finley had been one of its original trustees, and that his degree of doctor of divinity was only the second honorary degree ever conferred on an American by a British university. The doctor was a master Latinist. In the circumstances Benjamin's Latin could not have been so bad as he himself thought it was, and at college he was forced to improve both his Latin and his Greek. The original charter of the college, in 1746, had guaranteed religious freedom and promised instruction "in the Learned Languages and in the Liberal Arts and Sciences."

The Rev. Samuel Davies, who was president of the college while Benjamin was a student, took the word "Liberal" seriously. He introduced worldly subjects into the curriculum, stocked the library with books on mathematics and Newtonian philosophy, favored English prose over Latin poetry, and allowed singing and organ music in the chapel service.

He at once recognized Benjamin's native gift as a writer of English and his talent for public speaking. Davies, an orator himself, encouraged and improved the talent.

President Davies also encouraged his students to keep a "Liber Selectorum," a book in which to copy favorite passages from the classics they read. "By recording those passages," Rush wrote later, "I was led afterwards to record facts and opinions" in a "Commonplace Book." In doing so, Rush anticipated the advice of the poet William Wordsworth, who said a commonplace book should be "Abundant in observation and sparing of reflection." Rush's commonplace book is factual, reportorial and, for the most part, highly serious, but it also proves that he had an eye for the colorful personality and a sense of the humorous, whimsical and ridiculous.

In one place, for example, he wrote, "To be a gentleman subjects one to the necessity of resenting injuries, fighting duels and the like, and takes away all disgrace in swearing, getting drunk, running in debt..., etc.... [Gentlemen] are the greatest lyars in the world. They lie to their creditors, to their mistresses, to their fathers or wives, or to the public."

Rush also reported the wonders he beheld when he "went to see a 'learned pig.' He was a year old, was about 1/2 a foot high," and was even more precocious than eighteenth-century children.

Of course, these entries were made long after his college days. But they serve to show that neither the rigorous and sober training he received, nor the more rigorous and sober discipline and work schedule he imposed on himself in later years could kill his sense of humor or his unflagging interest in everything around him, including human frailty and animal genius.

WHEN Benjamin entered college, one of the trustees, a young lawyer named Richard Stockton, lived on a Princeton estate called "Morven." Mr. Stockton turned out to be "the most distinguished member of the first class" graduated from the college. He became a member of the New Jersey Provincial Council, a judge of the colony's supreme court, a member of the Continental Congress, and a signer, with Rush, of the Declaration of Independence.

More important, so far as Benjamin was concerned, was that on March 2, 1759, the spring of Benjamin's matriculation, a daughter was born to Mr. and Mrs. Stockton. She was named Julia. Four years later alumnus Benjamin Rush, back in Princeton for the year's commencement exercises, carried the little girl in his arms from the then new and now famous Nassau Hall to her home at Morven. A dozen years later he was to carry her *away* from Morven.

Since Richard Stockton was a lawyer himself, he may have had more to do with Benjamin's original decision to study law after graduation in September, 1760, than the record shows. When President Davies asked the new bachelor of arts what profession he intended to follow, Rush told him he "had been advised to study the law." Certainly his college mates, impressed by his oratorical skill, favored the choice. So did President Davies, who said that his star orator would "make a better figure at the bar, than in the walks of a hospital."

But the best laid schemes often go awry. After a Philadelphia lawyer had agreed to take him on as an apprentice, Rush visited an old schoolmate in Maryland. On his way back to Philadelphia he stopped for a few days with Dr. Finley and told him of his choice of profession. The doctor looked grave.

"I am sorry to hear it," he said.

"Why, sir?" Rush asked. "It is one of the honored professions, and I am advised that my ability as a speaker makes it a natural choice."

Dr. Finley thought this over for a moment. "It is a profession, yes," he said, "and some men make it an honored one. But there are others who succumb to its temptations, and dishonor not only the profession but themselves. A lawyer is paid to win cases, and sometimes the pay looms larger than the merits of the case. Some lawyers are like parliamentary debaters who are carried away by their own eloquence in a bad cause. Your very eloquence, Benjamin, is a danger, for you are headstrong and often too sure that you are right." The doctor smiled to soften the blow he had given. "Forgive me if I have been harsh in my judgment of both you and the law."

"Certainly, sir," Rush said. "I respect your judgment more than that of any man I know. I am only sorry that you think me headstrong and — " He hesitated.

"Self-righteous?"

Rush's face reddened. "Yes, sir," he said.

The doctor smiled again. "It is a weakness I hope you will outgrow. Let me see, you are not yet fifteen, isn't that right?"

"Yes, sir," Rush said, and looked questioningly at his uncle. "May I ask what profession you think best for me?"

Dr. Finley frowned thoughtfully. "You are a close observer, Benjamin," he said, "and a painstaking workman. You also have a kind and gentle heart. These are qualities that grace a doctor of medicine. I think you ought to consider the medical profession." He was silent a moment. "But before you determine on anything, set apart a day for fasting and prayer, and ask God to direct you in your choice of a profession."

Later Rush was "sorry to say" that he neglected the latter part of this excellent advice, but yielded to the former, and proceeded to obtain a letter of recommendation from Mr. Davies to Dr. John Redman to become his pupil.

6. Freshman in Medicine

THE GREAT CHOICE WAS MADE, but with misgivings. There were two professions in which Benjamin's eloquence would have been in his favor — law and divinity. His flirtation with the law was born of friendly suggestion. His childish announcement in the smithy near the river that he intended to be a preacher was born of the air he breathed.

Some time after he had become apprenticed to Dr. Redman in February, 1761, he wrote to a former college mate: "Who knows, but that my heart may be sufficiently changed to enter that holy calling." His only excuse for his choice of medicine was his "aversion to the study of law" and his "incapacity for that of Divinity."

Perhaps his misgivings were just freshman fright. Perhaps they were deliberately instilled by his "preceptor," Dr. John Redman. At any rate, Redman's first talk with his apprentice was not designed to put him at ease.

The morning after Benjamin had moved into the doctor's house, Redman summoned him into his "shop." It was like being summoned to the fount of all medical wisdom. Redman was nearly thirty-nine, his apprentice a boy just turned fifteen. Redman himself was a product of the reigning apprentice system. Later he had practiced a year in Bermuda, studied for a year at the medical Mecca of Edinburgh University in Scotland, received his M.D. from Leyden University in Holland, and done postgraduate work in Paris and London. Since its founding ten years before, he had been consulting physician at the Pennsylvania Hospital, the first hospital in America.

Redman's summons, brought by a servant, wakened his apprentice from a deep, early-morning sleep. Benjamin leaped out of his warm feather bed into what seemed a sub-zero winter temperature. His fingers, trembling as much from anxiety as from the cold, fumbled at the buttons of his nightgown. In the pitch darkness he pawed at his clothes on a chair near the bed, barked his shin on a footstool, stubbed his toe against a bedpost, tramped all over his shoes, and finally got into his clothes.

He decided not to wash up. The water in his pitcher, even if he could find the pitcher, was probably frozen solid. He just combed his hair with his fingers, and floundered down the hallway to the door of Redman's shop, or consulting-room.

When he entered the room, it was like jumping into the tropics straight from the North Pole. The Franklin stove was going great guns. The doctor, his face haggard with fatigue, was sitting at his table reading a book by the light of three candles. Benjamin closed the door softly behind him and waited to have his presence acknowledged. For some moments the doctor continued reading, then placed a marker in his book and laid it aside.

"Come!" he said impatiently without looking round. "Sit by the table."

Benjamin hurried to a chair at the end of the table to the doctor's left and sat down, his back stiff as a ramrod.

"Is it your custom to sleep all day, young man?" Redman snapped.

"No, sir," Benjamin said, "but I *am* a powerful sleeper."

"As my apprentice — if you remain my apprentice — you will learn to live on very little sleep."

"Yes, sir."

Redman looked at him coldly. "I am not sure that I was wise in accepting you," he said. "Oratory, they say, is your only claim to fame. A sickroom, the walks of a hospital, a surgical theater are places of silence — except, of course, for screams of agony and groans. Eloquence has never set a broken leg or charmed away a fever. If you study under me you will be seen but not heard, speak only when spoken to. Is that clear?"

"Yes, sir."

"After you have learned enough to ask sensible questions," Redman conceded, "you may ask questions." He passed his hand over his face and looked sternly at the apprentice. "You will master every book in my library and every other medical work you can lay your hands on. In particular, you will become letter-perfect in the works of Dr. Thomas Sydenham of England and Dr. Hermann Boerhaave of Holland, the gods of my idolatry. You are fortunate in having studied Latin under the finest Latinist in America, your uncle Dr. Finley. He tells me, however, that your Latin leaves something to be desired. President Davies concurs. But with extraordinary application you may survive. I do not expect you to become the equal of one of my late apprentices, John Morgan, who is now studying at Edinburgh after six years under me, but you may one day be worthy of carrying his bag."

This onslaught did not seem to call for comment, so Benjamin suffered himself merely to be seen.

"It is not my intention this morning," Redman continued,

"to introduce you into the mysteries of my calling. Your ignorance would make it a waste of breath. I simply want to
let you know what you are in for." The doctor gazed at the
ceiling as he went on. "The human body and its ailments are
a hutch of mysteries — a very few solved, the rest unsolved
and perhaps insoluble. Practitioners of medicine have been
groping in the dark for scores of centuries, stumbling on a
fact or a truth, now and then, but mainly stumbling over
their own feet. We try this, that and the other hoped-for
remedy. The patient dies. Or he lives, and the physician
jumps to the conclusion that the last-used drug or herb or
whatever was responsible for the recovery. But in most cases
the remedy last used was used just before Mother Nature ef-
fected the cure herself." He lowered his eyes from the ceiling. "Does that discourage you?"

It did, and Benjamin hesitated to admit it, but honest John
Rush's spirit was standing at his side. "A little, sir," he said.

"If it didn't," Redman said, "I would dismiss you this in-
stant as an indifferent wretch. It discourages me, too, but
medicine is above all the art of learning to live with dis-
couragement and to keep on going — groping through darkness and superstition, through filth and misery and death."
He closed his eyes and rubbed them, as if rubbing away their
fatigue. "The eyes," he went on, "are our most reliable instru-
ment. Dr. Finley tells me you are a good observer. That's
good. A doctor must observe with *all* his senses — with his
his nose, which can smell out measles; with his fingers, which
can feel a pulse; with his tongue, which can distinguish a poison from a harmless substance. Use them, sharpen them.
Learn to keep them awake when you cannot remember when
you last lay in a bed."

In the furious heat of the room Benjamin had grown
drowsy and was about to yawn. Now he made a heroic effort to
look wide awake. He looked sympathetically at Redman's
drawn face and weary eyes.

John Redman, M. D.

"That is the only way," the doctor went on, "to stay ahead of the vast army of charlatans who shamelessly practice what they call medicine. They outnumber trained physicians by some ten to one. They have another advantage over us — they are skilled peddlers. They promise the moon to their gullible victims. Their concoctions of cobweb, chicken feathers and calf's foot, they say, will cure everything from ingrown toenail to lockjaw. They are criminals, but there is no way to bring them to justice. They have as much or as *little* legal right to practice as we have. In our own province, as in the others, no one is licensed to practice medicine. I'm not, no doctor is, and where there is no legal right to practice real medicine there is immoral license to practice quackery and witchcraft." The doctor grimaced. "A plague on all their houses!"

The fire had died down a little, and in the more temperate climate Benjamin didn't have to pretend to be awake. He was. He could hear his stomach growling from emptiness. Perhaps Redman heard it, too. He got up, walked to the door and opened it.

"Sophia!" he cried. "Fetch our breakfast."

Leaving the door open, he went back to his chair and sat down.

"A medical apprentice," Redman began again, "is both a low menial and an exalted follower in the steps of Hippocrates." He looked at Benjamin. "Do you know him?"

"Vaguely, sir."

"He is the patron saint of medicine, the first known doctor to make good use of the brain and senses God gave him." He waved his hand toward his bookshelves. "I have his aphorisms here. You will read them — if you have enough Greek — and if you ever take a degree in medicine, which is problematical, you will take his oath before you begin to practice."

A young girl entered the room carrying a tray, set it on the table before the doctor, and left the room, closing the door behind her. Redman poured two cups of steaming tea and placed one, with a bowl of porridge, in front of Benjamin.

"Help yourself to milk and sugar and bread and butter," Redman said. "I can't vouch for these preserves, but risk them if you like."

For a few moments they were both busy and silent. The doctor bit into a slice of bread and butter, and he scowled.

"The cow this butter came from evidently got into some foul weeds," he said. "We are both like to come down with the milk sickness." He spooned some milk from a pitcher and tasted it. "Not the same cow. This one had better taste in fodder." He poured milk on his porridge and passed the pitcher to Benjamin.

The apprentice was too hungry to heed his master's warning about the milk sickness and wolfed down six slices of bread and butter and preserves with his porridge. Redman barely tasted the porridge, then sipped his tea thoughtfully.

"You will accompany me on my rounds," he began again, "carry my bag, hold the bowl at bloodlettings, run errands, nurse the sick, take note of everything I do or say, and in the evening write down what you have learned or think you have learned." He nodded toward an apothecary's balance and mortar and pestle on the far corner of the table. "You will also be my apothecary."

Benjamin strangled on his third cup of hot tea. "Apothecary?" he ventured when the paroxysm was over.

"Apothecary," Redman repeated, "a knight of the mortar and pestle — as innocent of any knowledge of chemistry as he is of the topography of the dark side of the moon."

"Yes, sir."

"There is not a single professor of chemistry or professional apothecary in the colonies. That is both a curse and, in a financial sense, a blessing. The ordinary physician, or pill-roller, would starve to death if he depended on his fees. Much the greater part of his income is from the sale of prescriptions." He paused. "I urged John Morgan when he went abroad to fetch back a real apothecary when he returned. Morgan has courage. He will fetch back an apothecary. But when he does he will have our whole profession at his throat. I warned him."

He paused again, taking note of the ravages Benjamin had made on the bread and butter and preserves. "And now it is time to begin rounds. The sun must be nearly up. I think you had better wash the preserves out of your ears and get the hair out of your eyes."

BESIDES being observant, Benjamin was diligent. He learned fast, but it seemed to him that he learned mostly what to avoid doing. Some of the things to avoid were traditional home remedies, some the remedies of the quacks. It was often hard to tell them apart. But he learned that you couldn't cure worms in a baby by feeding it scrapings from a pewter spoon or cure yellow jaundice with a mixture of ivory comb scrapings and honey. A baby with whooping cough was no better off having a bag of little bugs ground-up alive hung around its neck or for having been passed three times through a horse collar. A baby might die of croup if all you did was tie the right foot of a mole around his neck with a black thread. A spider tied to the neck of a man with ague might survive, but not the patient. It was fruitless to tell someone bitten by a mad dog to "take one teaspoonful per day of a mixture of one ounce of burned pulverized tongue of a newborn colt, one scruple of old 'verdigrease,' mixed with calomel." Mumps did not disappear if you rubbed the swellings against a pig trough. An aching tooth ached worse if you picked it with a splinter from a tree struck by lightning, a coffin nail,

the needle used in making a shroud, or the nail of the middle
toe of an owl.

No, you rolled your own pills as prescribed by Dr. Redman. At first you didn't know much about what you were doing, but you rolled the pills and hoped for the best. You also
became convinced that apprentices should all go through a
systematic course in chemistry.

BENJAMIN's apprenticeship lasted five and a half years — until July, 1766. "During this period," he wrote in his *Autobiography*, "I was absent from his [Redman's] business but
eleven days, and never spent more than three evenings out of
his house." Within a year Redman's confidence in Rush was
so complete that he often left his practice, the largest in the
city, to his favorite apprentice.

Benjamin's personal misgivings about the study of medicine soon disappeared despite "an uncommon aversion from
seeing such sights as are connected with its practice." His ex-
treme piety and moral fervor were not affected by his profession.

His tireless study and reading must have pleased his "sincere friend and father" Dr. Redman. He reread his "school
authors, especially the *Greek Testament* and *Horace*," read
many new things in Latin, medical works in particular,
though he begged off from corresponding in Latin with a
friend, and not only read Hippocrates but translated his
aphorisms into English. Because of the many Germans in the
city, he even planned to learn German, but postponed the
project. He was too busy.

During his apprenticeship Rush witnessed much turmoil
in the medical world. Its principal figure was Dr. William
Shippen, Jr., a graduate of the College of New Jersey, who
had taken his M.D. at Edinburgh. After returning to Philadelphia, Shippen announced the first course in anatomy to be

given in America. His students — of whom Rush was one of
the ten regulars — dissected human bodies, which Philadelphians felt to be a blasphemous prying into God's secrets.
Shippen said the cadavers were those of suicides and ex-
ecuted criminals, "with now and then one from the potter's
field," but his opponents accused him of stealing the bodies
from graveyards. Shippen's life was threatened, and stones
crashed into his dissecting-room.

Rush also attended lectures in *materia medica,* given by
Dr. Morgan. John Morgan had fulfilled all of Redman's expectations. He had been brilliant at Edinburgh, where he
received his M.D. in 1763, and had lectured triumphantly in
Europe for some two years. But his return to Philadelphia
was the signal for further turmoil. Like Shippen, who had
married a Lee of Virginia, Morgan was an elegant man. Philadelphians scoffed at him for carrying a parasol to fend off
sun and rain, and Shippen went berserk when Morgan established the Medical College of Philadelphia, the first of its kind
in America, and lectured under its auspices. Shippen claimed
that Morgan had stolen the idea from him during a talk they
had had in Edinburgh in 1761. Morgan replied that the co-
operative plan Shippen had then proposed had not been a
plan for "a collegiate undertaking" but only a "private
scheme" for medical lectures by Morgan and anatomical
lectures by Shippen.

But that wasn't all. Morgan brought a well-trained apothecary from England, as Redman had predicted he would, and
recommended that all physicians send their prescriptions to
him. A raw apprentice, he said, could not possibly be a good
pharmacist, and rolling pills was unworthy of a doctor, who
should confine himself to the role of scientist. Doctors
gnashed their teeth, and Shippen led the attack on Morgan
for trying to snatch away the profession's pill-rolling profits.

Rush rooted for Morgan from the sidelines during the apothecary fracas.

Early in September, 1766, with Susanna's help and a little borrowing of money, Rush was off on the next leg of his educational journey — aboard the *Friendship,* bound for Edinburgh via Liverpool and London.

 7. Edinburgh

THE CROSSING OF THE NORTH ATLANTIC was rough on the *Friendship* and on Rush. Almost lost off the coast of Ireland and wrecked on the coast of Wales, the ship at last made Liverpool on November 3, 1766.

As soon as he was ashore, Rush got off a letter to Benjamin Franklin in London. "As I have the happiness of being born in the province where you have resided many years," the letter said, "I was anxious to come under your patronage." At Edinburgh, that is. In the envelope he enclosed letters of introduction and recommendation from some of Franklin's friends at home. He then took the stage for Edinburgh.

Franklin at once dispatched letters to the eminent Edinburgh physician, Sir Alexander Dick, assuring him of Rush's "fine character, industriousness and good morals," and to Dr. William Cullen, professor of materia medica at the Medical

College. By the time Rush presented himself to Dr. Cullen, Franklin's letter and one from Dr. Morgan in Philadelphia had already reached him.

"Welcome to Edinburgh, Mr. Rush," Cullen said. "Dr. Morgan speaks highly of you, and when the great Dr. Franklin tells me that you will do honor to the College, I am confident that your stay among us will be a happy and fruitful one."

"They are too kind, sir," Rush said. "I can only hope that I will not fall too far short of their expectations. It is a privilege to be able to study under a great scholar and physician like yourself, sir. Dr. Morgan — "

Cullen chuckled. "I think we had best stop making speeches to each other, Mr. Rush." He shook Rush's hand and waved him out of his study. "Be off about your business. Let us hope we can live up to our friends' puffing."

RUSH'S first business was to have a look at Edinburgh. He found that though its area was only two-thirds that of Philadelphia, it had twice as many people — about 80,000. Most of them were crowded, family upon family, into tall, hivelike houses built so close together that yards and gardens were rare. Also rare was any neighborly communication between families.

Sanitation was shocking to a man used to the cleanliness Franklin had introduced into Philadelphia. "All their filth of every kind," Franklin had reported of the Edinburghers, "is thrown out of their windows." This ritual was practiced after ten at night. The filth was collected in the morning. Unwary late evening pedestrians thus ran the risk of being what was called "naturalized."

"The moral order which prevailed among all classes of people" Rush found exemplary, however. At night the streets were quiet, on Sunday the churches crowded. No one played cards. "Large evening companies" danced instead of being stupidly silent or insipidly conversational. The "genteel" rarely swore. "Common people" rarely got drunk.

The medical school was sober and serious. Once his studies began, Rush spent his days and most nights in the kind of unremitting toil he had become accustomed to under Dr. Redman, who had endowed him with a spectacular capacity for hard work, which he never lost. Nor did he lose his stubbornness and tenacity of purpose. In his role as student, these three qualities were priceless.

By the end of his first year of study, he was uncompromising in his conviction that "The present era will be famous for a revolution in physic. The old doctrines of the blood, nerves, etc., are now exploded, and much more rational ones substituted." Among other doctrines exploded, he wrote, were one of Dr. Morgan's and one of Dr. Shippen's. "The theory of physic is like our dress, always changing, and we are always best pleased with that which is most fashionable."

Cullen's "system," which Rush was learning, was more a change of fashion than a revolution. But there was a real revolution going on, too — a revolution that was overthrowing a more than 2,000-year-old theory of disease.

This was the theory of "humors," originated by the ancient Greeks. The world, the Greeks believed, consisted of four elements — fire, air, water and earth. The human body, they thought, contained a comparable set of four fluids, or "humors," with qualities corresponding to those of the four elements. Yellow bile was in the liver. Blood had its source in the heart. "Phlegm" was in the brain. Black bile was in the spleen.

Health, said the Greeks, is a question of a nice balance among the four humors. An upset balance was a disease. To cure it, the physician had to somehow restore the balance.

This old Greek theory was hard to kill. But, even as early

as the sixteenth century, the great Swiss physician Paracelsus had rejected the "humors" theory. By the time Rush went to Edinburgh, the studies of the new physics and chemistry were discrediting it completely. One of the men responsible was the celebrated Dr. Joseph Black, professor of chemistry at Edinburgh. He was a pioneer in quantitative measurements and, among other things, had proved the difference between carbon dioxide gas, then called "fixed air," and "common air." Under Black's influence Rush fell in love with chemistry.

Increasingly important as the new physics and chemistry were, the "humors" doctrine was nonetheless still dominant in medicine throughout the Western world, including America. Rush's first medical teacher, Redman, was a typical exponent of this doctrine.

The high priest of the doctrine had been the Dutch physician Hermann Boerhaave, who died in 1738. Boerhaave was "the teacher of all Europe." He was not an experimental scientist — what doctor was? — but a clinician, who did his teaching in his twelve-bed clinic, a method widely adopted after his example. Basing his therapy on the "humors," he claimed that disease arose from "morbid acrimonies" (bad matters) in the blood. These could be eliminated through the urine or pores or by mild bloodletting. This was, of course, pure "rational" speculation, not science. Nobody, including Boerhaave, had ever established the existence of morbid acrimonies. Hence nobody could prove that they caused disease.

By the time Rush got to Edinburgh, Cullen was in the process of substituting his own system of "rational" speculation for Boerhaave's. His theory was that the cause of disease was the malfunctioning of the nervous system, which was the source of life. Sometimes, he said, excessive nervous activity caused fever and spasm of the blood vessels. During the following "cold fit," or chill, the brain released too little energy and caused weakness.

A fever patient, according to Cullen, should have a scanty diet, cathartics, and cool air. These, together with blood-letting, would reduce the spasm. During the succeeding "cold fit" it was necessary to restore the energy lost during the fever. The patient should then be given nourishing food and stimulating drugs, the kind depending on which one of Cullen's list of 1,387 diseases the patient had.

Just as he had fallen in love with chemistry under Dr. Black, Rush went for Dr. Cullen's "system" like a robin for a worm. Cullen made his doctrine all the more appealing by lecturing in English instead of Latin.

AFTERWARDS it is always easy to see the folly of an event. Now that we know what scientific medicine is, we realize that the "systems" of both Boerhaave and Cullen were merely "rational," metaphysical hunch-playing, with hardly an established fact to go on except the few turned up by trial and error.

Medicine in those days lacked the scientific tool without which its problems cannot be solved. It was more than a century later that one of Rush's hunches was proved scientifically by a *controlled* clinical experiment. The *control* is the heart of scientific method. One of the most beautiful examples of its use was that of Dr. Walter Reed, after whom the famous hospital in Washington, D.C., is named. In 1900 Reed headed a commission to investigate an epidemic of yellow fever among American troops in Cuba.

Reed proved his hypothesis by showing that a *control group* of well persons — sleeping in the filthy bedding of yellow fever victims, but *not* bitten by the microbe-carrying mosquito — did *not* contract the disease. Those who did contract it lived in a clean, airy house and slept in clean bedding, but were allowed to be bitten by microbe-carrying mosquitoes that were *known* to have bitten yellow fever victims.

William Cullen, M. D.

What causes disease? Like every medical student or physician worth his salt, Rush was seeking the answer. Not all of his searching was done at the medical school. Through his growing reputation as a man of intellect and social grace, he was invited into the best homes in Edinburgh. Thus, he met a number of people famous in literature, the arts and philosophy.

He sometimes dined in the home of Sir Alexander Dick, one of the physicians to whom Franklin's letters had introduced him. One evening at Sir Alexander's he met a man who was an expert on the problem of causation in general. This was David Hume, a canny Scottish historian and philosopher. When dinner was over and the ladies had withdrawn, Rush sat at the table while Sir Alexander and Hume enjoyed a glass or two of port wine. Hume turned to Rush.

"You are a student of Dr. Cullen's, I presume, Mr. Rush," he said.

"Yes, sir."

"I believe Dr. Cullen attributes disease to the malfunctioning of the nervous system," Hume said.

"Yes, sir," Rush said. "At last the cause of disease is known."

"That is comforting. I have always been unhappy about Dr. Boerhaave's 'morbid acrimonies' in the blood. They smack of fiction, like the Scottish ghost in *Macbeth,* the ghost of Banquo. They seem but figments of the imagination."

"Exactly, sir, but there is nothing imaginary about nervous energy."

"Quite right," Hume agreed, "but I am curious to know how Dr. Cullen goes about proving that an excess of nervous energy causes fever."

Sir Alexander cleared his throat. "Now, David, don't get on your hobbyhorse," he said. "Mr. Rush may be frightened by it, as Macbeth was frightened by Banquo's ghost."

Hume looked at his host with an assumption of wide-eyed innocence. "Surely, sir, you would not prevent me from improving my mind. I am a student, too, you know." He turned back to his quarry. "How does he prove it, Mr. Rush?"

Rush had heard of the formidable David Hume, and was beginning to fear a trap. But if he was ever going to lead a crusade under Dr. Cullen's banner, a little practice crusading wouldn't hurt. "Well, sir," he said, "excess nervous energy always accompanies a fever."

Hume nodded. "I see — just as the bride always accompanies the bridegroom to the altar. But would you say the bride *causes* the bridegroom?"

Rush and Sir Alexander laughed. Hume smiled benignly.

"Or would you prefer to say," he went on, "that love, which always precedes the march to the altar, is the cause of the march?"

"I would prefer that, yes, sir," Rush said, laughing again, a little nervously.

Recovering his composure, he added, "I'm afraid I must, sir, but in medicine and the other sciences men have to believe that one event causes another event. I mean for practical reasons."

"Good!" Sir Alexander exclaimed. "Let's see you get out of that, Mr. Philosopher."

HUME was one extra-curricular Edinburgh educational influence. John Bostock was another. Despite Rush's own testimony, Bostock's influence was not immediately effective. An incubation period was necessary.

Rush and Bostock were not only fellow medical students but, they happily discovered, fellow descendants of men who had fought under that rough old king-hater Oliver Cromwell. "I had been taught," Rush wrote in his *Autobiography*, "to consider [kings] as essential to the political order as the

sun is to the order of the solar system." Bostock changed all
that, he went on, and showed him "the absurdity of hereditary power." It will be clear shortly, however, that he found
his awe of British royalty not entirely dissipated by Bostock's
arguments.

At any rate, while he was in Edinburgh he was not above
dropping names of the hereditary Scottish nobility. He had
come from home, he said in a letter to a Philadelphia friend,
"with a resolution to avoid forming connections with persons
of great distinction," but he now confessed that he had "the
honor of being intimate in the family" of David Leslie, 6th
Earl of Leven and 5th Earl of Melville. He admired the Earl's
moral and intellectual qualities, "contracted a particular acquaintance" with his eldest son, and during his stay with the
family in the summer of 1768, he fell in love with Lady Jane,
the eldest daughter, in the course of "many fine philosophic
walks."

He probably did not go so far as a proposal. One reason
was doubtless Lady Jane's awesome social eminence. Another
was his family's resolute opposition to his marrying anyone
at all "for eight or ten years to come." His sisters, Rachel
and Rebecca — both now widowed and with children — had
to be taken care of, and their brother Benjamin would have
to help in their support. His love for Lady Jane, then, could
at best be a practice exercise.

His family had seen to it that an earlier and evidently a
more serious romance at home was to have no future. In this
case the young lady was Mary Fisher, called "Polly." Before
he had met Lady Jane, Rush had written his friend Thomas
Bradford that prior to receiving the no-marriage orders,
from the family he had been about to ask his mother for permission to correspond with Polly. After the orders he gave
up. Now he was afraid that Polly would charge him with
inconstancy. "But oh!" he exclaimed to Bradford, "Did the

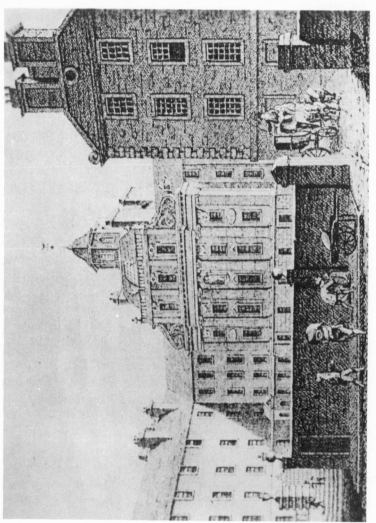

The Royal Infirmary, Edinburgh

blessed creature know what pangs of love she has cost me. Did
she know how often I have walked up and down my room for
whole nights together since I came to Scotland, thinking
upon nothing but her."

Bradford, a true friend, hastened to save Rush from a lifetime of remorse and Polly from the ravages of a broken heart.
Seven months later he married Polly himself. When Rush returned to Philadelphia, the rescuer and the rescued all remained fast friends. Rush could not have spent too many
nights thinking of the unattainable Polly, for he was working
as only Rush could work and taking his first steps in original
research. One project was his doctoral thesis on the digestion
of food in the stomach. When food is pumped out of the
stomach or thrown up, tests show it to have an acid quality,
that is, to be sour. Is digestion, then, Rush asked, a process
of fermentation?

To find out he took heroic steps. He was his own guinea
pig. Three hours after dinner he swallowed an emetic to
eject the food from his stomach. Tests showed the food to be
sour. Then, before dining on beef, bread, peas and beer, he
swallowed five grains of an alkaline salt to neutralize acid.
The food he again ejected from his stomach was again acid.
Substituting water for beer and veal for beef made no difference. The ejected food was again acid. Next time he ate
chicken, cabbage and unleavened instead of raised bread.
The result was the same as before. "From these facts thrice
repeated," he concluded, "an inference was drawn, that the
aliment in the human stomach, in the course of three hours
after being swallowed, undergoes acid fermentation."

Today we know that his conclusion was wrong. The
stomach does not ferment food the way yeast ferments malt
in a beer vat. Stomach enzymes, which help to digest food,
were not discovered for decades after Rush's gastronomic or-
deal. Though wrong in its conclusion, Rush's Latin thesis,

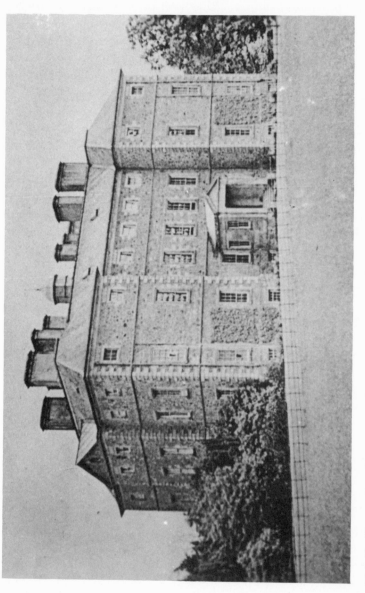

Melville House, Fifeshire, Scotland, Country Home of Rush's friends, William and Jane Leslie, children of The Earl of Leven

De Coctione Ciborum (Digestion of Food in the Stomach)
was a smashing success. Nearly fifty years later, it was still
possible for a famous London physician, Dr. John Lettsom,
to write that the thesis was "a performance so accurate, and
so ingenious and lucid in diction, as to have placed him in a
prominent and honourable point of estimation in that celebrated school [Edinburgh]."

Rush received his M.D. degree in June, 1768. That summer, while living with Lord Leven and his family, he attended a series of special lectures at the Medical College. Afterward, he obtained his family's permission to spend a year in
London and Paris. He had much studying to do yet and many
famous hospitals to observe. He also wanted to meet some of
the men in England and France whose names rang loud in
the world of intellect and culture. Besides, like any other
tourist, he had some sight-seeing to do.

8. London and Paris

BENJAMIN RUSH, M.D., AGE TWENTY-TWO, arrived in London in September, 1768. He took a furnished room in the Haymarket district near the Middlesex Hospital, where he was planning to attend lectures.

Besides instruction in the hospital, he was lucky in being able to attend a school in the home of the famous brothers, John and William Hunter, both anatomists and surgeons, who trained British doctors in dissection and surgery. One day an instructor named William Hewson, who was dissecting at Rush's side, settled an anatomical question that had long been in dispute. With singular skill, Hewson demonstrated by dissection that turtles and fishes have lymphatic vessels — channels through which fluids from the tissues and digested food from the intestines are carried to the blood. For the young American scientist who witnessed it, this historic demonstration was worth the cost of tuition.

Another medical development that excited Rush at this time was Daniel Sutton's simplified and successful method of smallpox inoculation. To bring about artificial active immunity to the disease, Sutton infected subjects by making a small puncture instead of a large gash. On his return to Philadelphia, Rush was to popularize this method, which made Sutton famous for more than a quarter of a century. It was only after Edward Jenner, in 1796, began infecting subjects with the equally effective but harmless cowpox instead of smallpox that Sutton's name suffered eclipse.

As an apprentice, Rush had realized that pill-rolling could be done properly only by one trained in chemistry. Ever since his first unhappy days with Redman's mortar and pestle, he had been determined to make himself master of the subject, and under Dr. Joseph Black he had received the best training available. Dr. Morgan, moreover, had given him hope that the professorship in chemistry at the Philadelphia Medical College would be held open for him until his return after he had taken his M.D. Morgan had continued to encourage the hope, and in January, 1769, Rush had written to thank him for the pains he had taken to secure the appointment.

But still, during an otherwise happy and interesting five-month stay in London, Rush was in doubt and worried about getting the position. Dr. Redman, a trustee of the College of Philadelphia and thereby also of the Medical College, had told Morgan — who had relayed the disheartening news — that their young protégé was not to take the professorship for granted. Later Redman wrote directly to Rush that to be appointed he would have to submit satisfactory testimonials concerning his qualifications.

Rush wrote Morgan that he himself had no doubt about

his ability to teach chemistry "with confidence and ease." He was "surprised at Dr. Redman's behavior." When he had written to Morgan back in January, Rush had been sure of his support, but Morgan, too, had grown chilly after Rush's thesis was published. The chilliness was due to the position of Morgan's name in the list of seven, to whom Rush dedicated the thesis. The list read, in order: Benjamin Franklin, Joseph Black, John Redman, William Shippen, John Morgan, Johnathan Smith (a college mate), and Jacob Rush.

Morgan proved touchy about his name appearing after his enemy Shippen's. Some two months before he left Edinburgh, Rush had tried to smooth things over, but he did it with the odd device of taking a slap at Redman. "I indeed," he wrote, "put Dr. Black before Dr. Redman, although the latter was my first master, but you know, sir, there are *teaching* and *ruling* masters." He made it clear that Dr. Black was the teaching master and Dr. Redman the ruling master, who was guilty of "base ingratitude" for the six years of mortar-pounding Rush had done. This explanation still left Morgan playing second fiddle to Shippen, and it is understandable that he did not relish the role. In any event, while in London, Rush continued to worry about the cool emotional climate in Philadelphia. About a month after he arrived in London he wrote that he hoped to relieve Morgan of his chemistry lectures in the fall of 1769, but perhaps he was only whistling to keep up his courage.

MEANWHILE through generous letters, Morgan introduced Rush into the medical world of the city of London. Franklin's influence opened doors to the wider world of culture, where Rush moved in an exclusive circle of writers and painters. Benjamin West, a native of Pennsylvania and historical painter of George III, partially quenched Rush's un-

republican curiosity about the King, the royal family, and
the nobility. While in the company of Dr. Samuel Johnson he
met some of the members of that omniscient literary dicta-
tor's "circle." Among others were Sir Joshua Reynolds, the
celebrated painter; David Garrick, one of history's greatest
actors; and Oliver Goldsmith, author of *The Deserted Village* and *The Vicar of Wakefield.*

Rush was also introduced to Sir John Pringle, a leading
name in science and founder of modern military medicine,
and Sir John invited him to attend weekly medical meetings
in his home. Here, Rush reports, he dined and talked with
"large and highly polished companies." Rush admired
Pringle's tireless search for knowledge, but could not stomach
Sir John's politics. Polite and correct when talking on other
matters, Pringle was a terror when anyone mentioned American resentment of British rule. "Liberty!" he would cry con-
temptuously. "The happiest people I know are those who
enjoy it least." Such outbursts kept John Bostock's republicanism incubating in Rush's mind.

But further incubation was still needed. When Rush visited
the House of Lords he felt that he "walked on sacred
ground." The sight of the throne filled him with indescribable
emotions, and when he got permission from the guide to sit
in it he "was seized with a kind of horror" at his own temerity.
The House of Commons — "O! Cursed haunt of venality, bri-
bery, and corruption!" — was another matter. "This," he
thought, "is the place where the infernal scheme for enslaving America was first broached." He went and sat on the very
spot "where Mr. Pitt (alas! now Lord Chatham) stood when
he spoke in favor of repealing the Stamp Act" and repeated
part of the speech from memory.

Three months later he met a member of Parliament who
influenced his republicanism even more than Pringle's anti-
Americanism or his memory of Pitt's speech. This was John
Wilkes — a firebrand republican who set every conservative

British tooth on edge — including Dr. Samuel Johnson's, but who brought cheers from the American Sons of Liberty. Rush, together with several other Americans and off-beat Englishmen, dined with Wilkes in the Kings' Bench Prison, where he had been locked up for seven months for publishing, among other "libels," an attack on the ministry of William Pitt, Lord Chatham. But even Wilkes and his politically unorthodox guests drank a toast to "His Majesty and the Royal Family."

What with his studies and his active social life, Rush's five months in London passed quickly. When he had time to spare, he spent much of it in the then eight-year-old British Museum — among its books, art objects and science exhibits.

In February, 1769, he left London and crossed the choppy English Channel, bound for Paris — armed with a number of letters of introduction from Benjamin Franklin to Parisian celebrities. He had not been long in Paris before concluding that French medicine was so ill-developed that formal study would not be profitable for him. But he did visit all the public hospitals, and his most fruitful experiences in Paris were outside the medical and scientific world.

French intellectual circles were in philosophical and political ferment. The French Revolution, which was to shake the foundations of the Western European world, was still two decades away, but its guiding ideas were already being shaped and sharpened. In the salons of such men as Denis Diderot — friend of Voltaire — and the Marquis de Mirabeau, sharp and logical French minds were dissecting the notions that had long been considered the unshakable bedrock of economic and political thought. Like John Bostock, these thinkers rejected the idea of hereditary power. They kept hammering away with the kind of ideology that was soon to find its most memorable expression in the American Declaration of Independence. Rush listened, talked, and became further infected with republicanism.

One of Franklin's letters had introduced the young physician to Dr. Jacques Dubourg. Dubourg, in turn, introduced Rush at one of Mirabeau's salon gatherings. As in any other salon of its kind, Franklin's name was magic. Dubourg entered the door of the room where the usual intellectual debate was in high gear. "Look!" he shouted. "One of Monsieur Franklin's friends." Mirabeau ran across the room and grasped Rush's hand. "That is enough," he said in French.

Although at such functions Rush's republicanism developed still further, he could not resist the urge to have a look at Louis XV, "the well-beloved." He went to Versailles and saw the King at worship in his chapel. "He had a good eye," Rush observed, "and an intelligent countenance, and hence he was said to be 'the most sensible looking fool in Europe.' "

He also beheld an example of royal table manners. Along with some hundred other curiosity-seekers and tourists, Rush was watching the royal family dine in public. The Dauphin, son of Louis XV and father of Louis XVI, chewed for some time on a piece of meat, then took it out of his mouth, looked at it disapprovingly, and threw it under the table.

At times Rush believed that such manners, and other peculiarities of the French, whom he regarded as the most civilized of all people, were due to the fact that the French were in their second childhood. The fact that, like the American Indians, they painted their faces was supporting evidence of their return to savagery. At other times and in other moods he found evidence pointing in the opposite direction.

On March 25, 1769, Rush recrossed the Channel on his way back to London. During the coach trip from Dover to the capital, he got his first chance to practice his profession as a full-fledged doctor. As the coach rolled along, the coachman and passengers saw a woman lying beside the road on an old blanket. The coachman pulled up his team, and when the noise of the wheels stopped, they could all hear the woman moaning. Rush leaped out of the coach and ran to her. The symptoms were obvious, and he ran back to the coach.

"She is in labor," he cried to a woman passenger. "I am a doctor. Please come and help me."

Ten minutes later, with his fellow passenger's help, Rush had delivered the anguished woman of a baby boy. Soon the father arrived with two neighbors, whom he had brought to help, and took the infant away. Rush and another passenger helped the woman into the coach, which carried her to a nearby village. On the way the woman looked thankfully at the young doctor who had perhaps saved her own life and her baby's.

"What is your name, sir?" she asked.

"Dr. Benjamin Rush."

"I will always remember it," she said. "Are you going to London?"

"Yes."

"Please give me your address."

He did so, not knowing why she wanted it. He found out several years later that shortly afterward she had turned up at his rooming-house to thank him once again and to show him her son Benjamin.

On a black morning in the last week of May, Rush boarded the ship *Edward,* bound for New York. He had seen Great Britain and Europe for the first and last time. He was not fated to be a far traveler; he never got so far north as New England or so far south as Virginia.

The two-month voyage home was almost as stormy as the career that lay ahead of him, but moderate seasickness did not interfere with his inveterate habits of study. While abroad he had learned to read French, Spanish and Italian, and during the voyage he read an Italian novel borrowed from the captain. He also borrowed a German grammar and dictionary and made his long-delayed but evidently fruitless attempt to learn German. He also studied the famous law classic, *Blackstone's Commentaries,* and a book on Crown Law. Who knew? Maybe he would be a lawyer yet.

After disembarking on July 14, he spent two days in New York with his old school and college friend Ebenezer Hazard, later postmaster-general. He found New Yorkers less colorful than Londoners and Parisians and — an odd fact, considering the modern New York tempo — slower moving. After his visit, he took the stagecoach for Philadelphia. His days on the sidelines were ending. He was ready for the crusade under Dr. Cullen's banner, and prepared to battle for the professorship of chemistry at the Medical College. If Dr. Redman wanted a fight, he would have it.

9. Homecoming

THE FIRST TWO WEEKS IN PHILADELPHIA allowed Rush no
time for crusading or for the showdown with Redman on the
professorship. He was too occupied with the homecoming
welcome by his family and friends — including Tom Bradford and his wife Polly — and too busy getting settled in a
rented house on Arch Street near the docks. Jacob, now an
apprentice at law, moved in with him, and their sister Rebecca, still not remarried, became their housekeeper.

When Jacob could steal an hour or two from his studies,
he took Benjamin on long walks through the city to see new
sights and renew old memories. For Jacob, two years younger
and still only a law apprentice and a dyed-in-the-wool provincial, it was a pleasure to be seen in company with his
brother. After all, Benjamin was an Edinburgh M.D. and
looked it, Jacob thought. Besides, after a year among the

learned and polished nabobs of London and Paris, Dr. Rush
had an air of elegance and an indefinable world-shine about
him. When men as well as women turned and had a second
look at them — or was it only at Benjamin? — Jacob felt very
proud and more important.

Philadelphia was bigger and more important than it had
been three years earlier. Not too long afterward, a British
globetrotter was to note that Philadelphia was "perhaps one
of the wonders of the World . . . the first town in America . . .
that bids fair to rival almost any in Europe." Rush, now with
a practiced eye of his own, would have agreed.

The new shops with their lavish wares along Front and
Market Streets were one evidence of growing business, wealth
and importance. They were also evidence of the greater
trade going on with the Northern and Southern colonies,
with the Indians, and with the frontiersmen and settlers who
were steadily pushing into the back country, into the mysterious interior of the vast and unexplored continent.

The greater number of ships along the river wharves was
evidence of growing foreign trade. Coming in on the ships
from England were woolens, linens, brocades, velvets, wines,
paper, glass, paints, and indentured servants. From the Far
East came silks, spices, tea, and fine hard woods. From the
"sugar islands" of the Caribbean came sugar, molasses and
slaves. Going out on the ships were tobacco, lumber, furs,
wool, grain, and dried fish. All these signs of increasing business and trade made it easy for Rush to believe what his
brother told him — that many of his old friends and acquaintances were getting rich as merchants and traders.

The newly rich lived much as the rich had lived when
Rush, awestruck, had wandered the streets with his brother
James, now some years dead of the yellow fever. Shade trees
still graced the wide, impressive street entrances to the red-
brick houses with their beautiful doorways and expansive,

small-paned windows. The rear gardens were as expertly manicured as ever.

When Benjamin and Jacob passed these houses at night, through the windows they could see the large, luxurious open fireplaces, the crystal chandeliers and silver candelabra whose light revealed the tasteful imported wallpaper and rich tapestries, the mirrors and clocks, the upholstered chairs with carved woodwork, the fashionable Chippendale and Sheraton tables, breakfronts and secretaries, and at times even the polished floors and thick, rich, sound-muffling carpets. Above all, they caught glimpses of the elegant inhabitants and of their servants and slaves carrying great trays and salvers burdened with fine china and crystal and burnished pewter. Once they even saw a servant hustling somewhere with a foot-warmer on an oppressively hot midsummer evening. Jacob laughed.

"What in the world!" he exclaimed.

"It's for an old man or old lady with poor circulation," his doctor brother explained.

But these houses were modest compared with those of the very rich on the outskirts of town, forerunners of the "Main Line" estates of modern Philadelphia. Here the houses were mansions flanked with stables, smokehouses, wine and cider cellars, and workrooms where slaves and servants — mostly indentured in temporary slavery — churned butter, made candles and soap, and otherwise ministered to the comfort and luxury of their masters and mistresses.

These grand folks were the mainstay of the city's culture, a culture that diffused from Philadelphia throughout Pennsylvania and the Middle colonies. In 1743, two years before Rush was born, Franklin had established the American Philosophical Society. Even then he was able to say that "The first drudgery of settling new colonies is pretty well over, and there are many in every colony in circumstances which

A street scene in Philadelphia (Third and Market Streets)

set them at ease to cultivate the fine arts and improve the common stock of knowledge."

Now, in 1769 — and in the years to follow — these "Mainliners" and the somewhat less affluent rich of downtown Philadelphia were in even better circumstances and even more at ease to cultivate literature, music and the arts. They largely accounted for the city becoming the center of the newspaper, periodical, and book-printing industry. They helped to stock the reading room of Franklin's Library Company, and to oversubscribe the winter concerts given by visiting European musicians. They applauded the English actors in such plays as *Hamlet* and Goldsmith's *She Stoops to Conquer,* astutely billed as an edifying "Lecture on the Disadvantages of Improper Education."

Despite his outward assurance, the "Main Line" estates and the imposing houses downtown, somehow chilled Rush's heart. For all his education, for all his social status abroad, here at home he was only a gunsmith's and shopkeeper's son — on the outside looking in at all this luxury. On these estates, in these houses, he would find no field for a career in medicine. The door of family connections among the rich, open to other young doctors, was closed to him.

The two other regular doors were also closed. If only Franklin were in Philadelphia, perhaps his patronage would help, but Franklin was still in England. The last regular door was religious affiliation, but the Rushes now belonged to the small and divided Presbyterian Society, not to the large, wealthy and influential Quaker and Episcopalian congregations.

One day, on one of their walks, while his mind's eye was contemplating these closed doors, Rush turned to Jacob.

"Let's take a walk down by the river," he said.

"All right. Any particular place?"

"Yes, a smithy that James and I used to go to. It was still

there when I left." Rush paused. "I don't know why, but I felt at home down there."

"So do I," Jacob said. "I guess we've got the common touch."

"The common touch," Rush mused. "Well, if I don't have it, I'm afraid I'll have to cultivate it. It looks as if the poor will be my only patients." He looked at his brother. "You know I don't hold with the theories of Dr. Boerhaave."

"Are you telling *me?*" Jacob laughed. "But what have they got to do with the poor?"

"Nothing. But Boerhaave said, 'The poor are my best patients, because God is their paymaster.' His theories were wrong, but his heart was in the right place. I hope mine is."

Jacob put his hand on his brother's shoulder. "Don't worry, Benjamin. It is."

THE old smithy was no longer there. Its site was now covered by part of a big new warehouse. But the narrow streets and alleys were almost the same as ever. Here, for the first time, Rush felt that he had come home. His step quickened, and his jaw set in a stubborn line. He had as good training as any physician in Philadelphia. He could get along without the rich, the well-born and the educated.

He could not get along without the professorship, however. He needed the prestige it would bring, not to mention the satisfaction of teaching chemistry.

When he got home, he sat down and wrote a letter. It was addressed to the trustees of the College of Philadelphia, formally offering himself "as a candidate" for the professorship in chemistry at the Medical College. The date was July 31, 1769. It might have struck him as presumptuous that a man of only twenty-three should expect to be appointed to the first position of its kind in America — but it did not.

Rush was convinced that not even Dr. Morgan, who had

been giving the lectures in chemistry without a formal title, was better versed in the subject than he was. In addition to Dr. Cullen's support, he had another valuable testimonial.

Before he left London Rush had obtained a letter from Thomas Penn, the Royal Proprietor of the Province of Pennsylvania, who had purchased "a chymical apparatus" he wished to donate to the College. Penn suggested to Dr. Fothergill, an eminent London physician, that Rush carry the apparatus with him to Philadelphia. He also suggested to Fothergill that he write a testimonial letter which he enclosed with his own letter to the College. At any rate, Fothergill did recommend Rush — with certain mental reservations, expressed in a letter to a Philadelphia friend. To this friend he admitted that Rush had studied with "much diligence and success" but he was afraid the young man might be spoiled by having his talents too hastily recognized by his friends at home.

Before Rush submitted his formal application for the professorship, he had delivered the apparatus and Penn's letter with Fothergill's enclosed. They turned the trick. The next day, August 1, 1769, Rush was elected. The professorship was the first of his many "firsts" as a physician and man of American affairs.

 ## 10. The Young Doctor

THE SECOND BATTLE, HE RIGHTLY FEARED — the battle for patients under the Cullen banner — would be much bloodier and longer drawn out. Once more he strode forth along the wharves and waterways, into the little towns outside the city such as Southwark and Kensington — among the poor.

The terrain and people were familiar to Redman's former apprentice. Rush knew what to expect, and when he doctored as many as sixteen patients on a single morning and was paid by only one, he was not surprised or downcast. Or if he was, he soon remembered that he was no better than Cullen or Fothergill or Boerhaave, who had devoted their great talents to the poor with no greater financial reward.

"My natural disposition," he wrote as an old man, "made this mode of getting into business agreeable to me, for I had a natural sympathy with distress of every kind." The poor were grateful for his skill and faithful care. They realized that young Dr. Rush, with the stubborn jaw and intelligent, kindly eyes, who went everywhere on foot — carrying his apothecary's shop in his bag — was just about as hard up for money as they were. They paid when they could, and their doctor knew from experience that this was more than could be said for many of the wealthy people in the elegant houses. His patients paid all the more readily because of the doctor's reassuring bedside manner, a manner that was to become the most celebrated in America. His reputation and practice grew slowly but steadily because of his ever-increasing popularity with his patients.

One of the reasons for this popularity was Rush's use of the Suttonian method of inoculating for smallpox, which had so attracted him in England. Having only a small puncture made in their arms, his patients thought, was much better than "reeling and writhing and fainting in coils" at the prospect of bleeding from a gash like a saber wound. His patients also approved of his not forcing them to gag on a wide assortment of costly medicines. Like his master Cullen, his chief reliance was on diet and "medicinal" wines, made sufficiently disgusting to discourage intemperance.

Medical skill was not his only road to popularity. His "decent behavior in the time of Divine Service," observed by a sea captain in a Southwark church, brought the captain around. A prominent merchant had had dealings with his mother, and introduced Rush to many friends, as the young doctor who had studied under Doctors John and William Hunter in London. A widely known midwife, who liked his looks, methods and manners, sent him still other patients. And then there was his professorship, which brought him not only prestige and patients but also a small but regular income.

Like other trained physicians, Rush had to compete with

the quacks, who advertised in the newspapers. They were now plying their quackery in even greater numbers than during his apprenticeship. "Dr." Anderton, really a glazier, peddled everything from "worm plumbs" to "a fine water for the eyes." "Dr." Day, who had "his name over his door in brass letters," sold "a bottle and a box for a dollar each, that infallibly cures the worst of fevers and agues, or the worst rheumatisms." The sufferer could obtain these cures after either personal or mail order consultation and diagnosis. The dubiousness of the cures of this brigade of quacks was equalled only by the brigade's irresponsibility. There was no Food and Drug Administration and no medical association to keep them in line, no licensing requirements — present day measures to protect people from advertising slogans sometimes used to confuse and mislead the public. Any lie they could think up, any promise they made, enjoyed legal immunity.

Competition from quacks, however, was much more bothersome to physicians with mediocre training than it was to Rush, who had had the best. His main obstacle to a large as well as a lucrative practice was the hostility of his medical colleagues, almost all of whom practiced the Boerhaave system. They were angered by the belligerence with which he waved the Cullen banner, and by the stubborn and often tactless scorn he poured on Boerhaave's adherents. It was all the worse for Rush that among those offended were the oldest and best established medical men in the city. They were not amused, for instance, when they heard that in the presence of a number of medical students, at a dinner in his home, he had proposed the toast: "Speedy interment of the System of Dr. Boerhaave, and may it never rise again."

The Boerhaave men retaliated by denouncing and ridiculing the Cullen system as new-fangled and hare-brained. In the press and wherever doctors gathered, Rush was the cen-

ter of debate, attack and name-calling. Dr. Shippen in particular — perhaps in part because he remembered Rush's
support of Dr. Morgan in the apothecary war of 1765 — bitterly resented the younger man's arrogance. Evidence of
Shippen's bitterness appears in a letter Jacob Rush wrote to
Benjamin from London, in 1771. "I am sorry that Dr. Shippen has kept away students from attending your lectures. At
the same time, I am not at all sorry that you are at variance
with him. Better, infinitely better is it to be at eternal variance with a man of his cool malice and treachery."

Rush appeared unconcerned with Shippen's deep malice.
Unorthodox at the beginning, he was to remain so to the end.
Unorthodoxy was nevertheless expensive. Toward the end
of his life he could not recall a single patient referred to him
by his colleagues during his first seven years of practice.

In time, the brilliance of his propaganda and the success
of his practice began to convince the Philadelphia doctors that
Boerhaave was wrong and Cullen right. By then, however,
Rush had begun to take a dim view of Cullen and to put
forward his own "system." The old battle between Rush and
his colleagues roared on without interruption. The only
change was a change of banners. His enemies carried Cullen's.
Rush carried his own.

To the eighteenth-century patient — burning with fever,
shaking with chills — it did not much matter which banner
his doctor carried. When neighbors compared notes on the
treatment they were getting, they must have been hard put
to detect any difference between one theory and another, one
hunch and another — all untested by the methods of laboratory or clinical science we know today.

If a doctor was a Boerhaave man he believed that disease
was due to "morbid acrimonies" — bad matters. Therefore,
the blood had to be thinned and cleansed. The physician's

job was to prescribe the best means of expelling the sickly matter not only from the blood but from the stomach, bowels, kidneys, and skin. Obviously, then, his remedies were designed to induce vomiting, purging, sweating, salivating, and the loss of blood through blood-letting. But if the doctor was a Cullen man and believed that excess nervous energy caused disease and fever, he, too, used the same depleting methods and the same drugs and herbs as the Boerhaave man, though in somewhat less variety.

The practice of both medical schools was relatively ineffective, and understandably so. Neither knew anything about bacteria, infection, and contagion. Epidemics — including epidemics of the deadly smallpox and yellow fever — recurred with disheartening regularity. Every summer people suffered from dysentery and cholera morbus, germ-caused diseases of the intestines. Every winter they suffered from agues, severe sore throats, scarlet fever, diphtheria, and pneumonia. Knowing nothing about germs and the preventives and cures based on the science of bacteriology, doctors of both schools of thought relied on what Hume called "beliefs" and "notions" arrived at through repeated observations by means of their unaided senses. It is, therefore, not surprising that frequently both schools entirely missed the target.

Besides thorough training, to be a good doctor, then as today, required dedication, self-denial, courage, endurance, the efficient use of time, and powers of close and accurate observation. Dr. Finley had rightly said that Rush was a good observer. Rush himself, America's first epidemiologist, attributed much of his knowledge of epidemics to his observations among the poor, where the diseases appeared early and in a simple form. He was always careful to note the effects of medication and the right dosage.

Until 1775, Rush spent a great deal of time among the poor. "My shop," he wrote, "was crowded with the poor in the morning and at mealtimes." At other times, he hunted them out in their narrow streets and alleys, often climbing ladders to reach their leaky and drafty attics. When they had no chairs, he risked disease and vermin by sitting on their bedsides. "Nor did I hasten from these abodes of poverty and misery," he reported. "Where no other help was attainable, I have often remained in them long eno' to administer my prescriptions, particularly bleeding and glysters [enemas], with my own hands."

In the old days, under Redman, he had learned to budget his time carefully, and he never lost the habit. Unless called on an emergency case, he remained in his office until nine-thirty or ten in the morning preparing for the day's labor. "Scraps of time" during meals or between sick calls he used for light reading, letter writing, and minor chores not requiring concentration. Between seven and nine in the evening, when not seeing patients or attending meetings, he studied.

During the later hours of the night, he thought and read and did his serious writing. When his weary eyes were about to close over a book, he turned to writing. When his writing flagged, he returned to his book with renewed wakefulness and energy. When these devices failed, he would throw fresh wood on the fire and bake himself awake or step out onto the rear balcony facing the river and, in winter, freeze himself awake. He seldom went to bed before midnight. Often he heard the night watch cry "three o'clock and all's well" before snuffing out his candle.

In the earliest days when he made all his calls on foot, the slow going irked him, but it irked him even more to have to waste time in profitless conversation with people who stopped him on the street. Using a carriage saved time for thought, so he acquired a horse and carriage. Whenever he got an idea — while walking or driving or in the fruitful moments just before falling asleep — he jotted it down.

No idea ever got away. Nor did any significant observed fact escape his notebooks. Whenever ideas or facts seemed worthy of being shared with the world, he wrote articles on them for publication. In 1770, after only one year of practice, he published one on spasm of the windpipe. "Hives" — the old name for this form of croup — had been deemed to occur only in diphtheria and to result from a membrane blocking the larynx, often fatally. Many postmortem dissections forced Rush to disagree. He said he had found croup in other diseases and that it was due to a tightening of the windpipe, not to the formation of a membrane.

In the same year he achieved his second "first" in American science. This was his publication of the first chemistry textbook by an American author. Its title was *Syllabus of a Course on Chemistry*. Despite Shippen's efforts at sabotage, Rush's public lectures in chemistry were well received. The subjects were varied and popular; the effect of heat on liquids and solids, climate, the making and use of thermometers, methods of manufacturing gunpowder, the nature of mineral waters, volcanoes. The lectures were one of the first efforts to popularize science, and helped to spread Rush's reputation as a learned and respected member of the community.

The following year, three of his essays, entitled *Sermons to Gentlemen on Temperance and Exercise,* were printed anonymously. Their simply written, sensible advice is as sound today as it was then. Proper exercise, he said, promotes physical health, mental vigor, and longer life. Riding in carriages was desirable only for the aged and the otherwise decrepit. Dancing, he said, doubtless recalling his Edinburgh days, strengthens the body and inspires cheerfulness. Golf also makes you cheerful, and he recommended the game.

Also, in 1772, he was appointed physician at the Alms-

house, later the Philadelphia General Hospital. The dictionary definition of *almshouse* is "a house for the use of the
poor." Here Rush treated those who were too poor to live
even in the back street attics. The appointment, then, was
the logical climax of his early practice, and conclusively testified to the public's recognition of his faith. But this recognition was by now beginning to have more concrete results.
His cash income was growing. It was about time — if he ever
intended to forsake bachelorhood and assume the financial
responsibilities of marriage.

11. Two Loves and
a Marriage

ONE OF RUSH'S EARLY CHEMISTRY STUDENTS quaintly reported
that when the young bachelor arrived home, in 1769, he was
determined "not to perpetrate matrimony till he had extended his studies so far that a family would be no impediment
to his further progress." The word "perpetrate" reflects
Rush's conviction that a premature marriage would endanger
his future career.

The recollections of these early years as they appear in his
Autobiography, written when he was an old and distinguished
man careful of his reputation, are remarkably free from ref-
erences to women. He does not mention Polly Fisher, Lady
Jane or a girl he met in the spring of 1773.

This last girl was Sarah Eve, daughter of Oswald Eve, a
sea captain who had once been wealthy but had fallen on
evil days. Clearly it could not have been Sarah's wealth or

connections that attracted the hitherto determined bachelor of twenty-seven. It could only have been Sarah herself — a fashionably dressed, witty and imaginative beauty of twenty-three.

By 1773, his family had evidently outgrown its objection to a possible marriage. His mother, Susanna, was now re-married to a wealthy distiller — a circumstance that may account for the anonymity of her son's *Sermons to Gentlemen on Temperance and Exercise*. Rachel was also remarried and off the list of dependents. Rebecca, never to remarry, did not stand in the way, either.

Susanna, in particular, seems to have approved of Sarah Eve. She sometimes visited the Eve farm, some two miles from her own house in town. Sarah, attracted by the older woman's friendliness, often visited Susanna, and once even stayed overnight. However deep in thought or worn out from climbing ladders to poverty-stricken attics, Rush always happened to drop by to see his mother when Sarah happened to be there.

For the record these stops were purely accidental. Sarah Eve was just as surprised by them as Dr. Rush. At twenty-three Sarah was too young to know of her father's financial straits. She had not heard — even from such a prime source as Susanna — of Dr. Rush's growing popularity with his patients, of the grudging respect being wrung from his colleagues and of his probable future eminence. Or had she? At twenty-three was she old enough to know what a catch the coming young doctor would be?

When she looked at his bright, intelligent eyes, did she get an inkling of his future distinction? Did his resonant orator's voice fall pleasantly on her ears? Did she, like Jacob, notice the elegance of his dress and manner? No one knows. We only know that she often happened to be having tea with Susanna when the doctor happened to drop by.

One thing is certain: Rush had not read Sarah's diary and, therefore, knew only the Sarah Eve who was on her good behavior when at tea with his mother. Would he have been shocked at Sarah's diary entry asking herself "why such an exemplary man as the Rev. Jacob Duché should sit every day and have his hair curled by a barber"?

In 1773, a young lady should have been more reverent. She should also have been more dutiful than Sarah. She should not have been obliged to confess in her diary that she and her friend Anna had promised to come straight home from a shopping trip but had instead connived at having their cloaks and bonnets "taken off by force and locked up" in order to have tea with Betsy Guest.

In that decorous time a young lady should not have poked fun at the "foolish custom" of having girls "prance through the streets without hats or bonnets" in a child's funeral cortege. Even with such proper young men as "B. Rush, P. Dunn, K. Vaughan" helping Sarah herself carry the casket, the custom, Sarah thought, was still foolish. On this solemn occasion, with his face as long as a lantern, what would B. Rush have thought of Sarah's thoughts?

What would B. Rush have thought of Sarah's thoughts on a man's kisses — especially if he had known that the man in question was Dr. William Shippen? Sarah thought it was "a pity that the doctor is so fond of kissing, because kissing is attended with so many inconveniences; it decomposes the economy of one's *handkerchief,* it disorders one's *high roll,* and it ruffles the serenity of one's countenance."

Fortunately, Rush knew nothing of the diary and its improprieties. He only knew that Sarah was delightful. Her companionship refreshed him after grinding labors and long nights of study. Busy as he was, during the spring and summer of 1773, he always managed to find time for long walks with her through the city streets and in the countryside. Sometimes they walked to Mineral Point, about a half mile from the center of town. Here there was a mineral spring that, according to popular belief, worked curative miracles equal to those of the most unscrupulous quacks. "The place looked dreadful," Sarah wrote in her diary, "more like a tan-pit than anything else; there was a thick, chocolate-colored scum over it, but when you blow this on one side the water is clear." B. Rush induced her to taste it.

"Phew!" she went, making a face. "It tastes inky. If it were only black, someone could bottle it and sell it for ink."

Rush laughed somewhat reluctantly. He was not a quack, but he thought well of mineral springs and even wrote an article on the subject.

Sarah's diary does not reveal what she felt toward B. Rush, or Mr. Rush, as it sometimes refers to him. She made her most enthusiastic entry when, in the fall, she and her mother fell ill and Rush called on them, much concerned. "Are we not blessed with the best of friends!" the entry read.

At the time friendship was as far as the relationship went on either side, but his courtship continued all that winter and the next summer and fall. Then Sarah capitulated, and the wedding date was set for December, 1774. Not long after the engagement, however, Sarah fell ill again. She never recovered. Her death came only three weeks before the marriage was to take place.

At six Rush had been too young to feel the full force of the loss of his father, but he had been deeply affected by the death of his brother James. Now he had suffered his second great loss. He never mentioned Sarah Eve in writing, except in the tribute to her that he published anonymously in the *Pennsylvania Packet*. In it he said that her manners "were not put on, and laid aside, like a part of dress . . . Such were her unaffected displays of good sense, modesty, and good humour, that no one, I believe, ever left her without emotions of love, esteem, or admiration."

In the fall of 1775, nearly a year after Sarah's death, Rush

called on Dr. John Witherspoon, a Scottish minister, whom
he had persuaded to accept the presidency of the College of
New Jersey. Through him Rush renewed his acquaintance
with Richard Stockton, the lawyer whose four-year-old
daughter he had once carried from Nassau Hall to Stockton's
Morven estate in Princeton.

Julia was now a pretty, buxom girl of sixteen. Her dark
hair, piled high above a high forehead and oval face, fell in
ringlets down her neck. Julia's appearance must have struck
Rush favorably, but he failed to mention it in his *Autobiography,* written so long afterward that he may have forgotten
just how she did look as a girl. What he remembered was
her "taste and understanding." Julia liked Dr. Witherspoon's
preaching. "She said he was the best preacher she had ever
heard. Such a declaration I was sure could only proceed from
a soundness of judgment and correctness of taste seldom to
be met with in a person of her age."

Dr. Witherspoon's sermons, it seems, were not spell-binders
and were commendable only for "their uncommon good
sense and simplicity of style," standard eighteenth-century
virtues. Julia's taste for them clinched the matter for Rush.
When he got back to Philadelphia he wrote to the Stocktons
for permission to visit their daughter. His visits soon led
to a proposal, which was accepted. The marriage, performed
by Dr. Witherspoon, took place on January 11, 1776, at
Morven. After the ceremony, Rush took his young bride to
his home on Front Street, corner of Walnut.

"It would be ungrateful to heaven not to acknowledge
how much happiness God has bestowed upon me in a wife,"
he said in a letter to a friend in Scotland some years after
his marriage. "She would pass for a *good woman* in Scotland,
and for what the world calls a *fine woman* even in England."

Thomas Sully's portrait of her, painted when Julia was in
her fifties, bears out the words of her doting husband. The

Mrs. Benjamin Rush, Portrait by Thomas Sully

clear complexion and unwrinkled skin, seen in the painting, may be the artist's diplomatic idealization of the wife of a then world-renowned physician, but there can be no doubt of the portrait's essential truth. Under the lace bonnet, with its escaping ringlets of hair, the face is beautiful, gentle and serene. It reveals the same character that can be read in her letters — and in her husband's, which might otherwise seem to be the distortions of a blind devotion.

During the summer after the marriage, Julia's health made it necessary for her to retire to Morven for a rest. In her absence Rush, busier and more preoccupied than ever, because of the onrushing course of the Revolution, returned to Front Street one day to write her everything he had seen and heard during the day — "when alas! the first steps I took in passing through the entry convinced me of my mistake. A melancholy silence reigns through every apartment of our house. Every room and piece of furniture proclaims that you are gone, and sympathizes with me in lamenting the absence of their mistress."

These words cannot be explained as merely the understandable outburst of a man scarcely six months married. Throughout his life separation from Julia left him unbearably lonely, almost anguished.

It is not so clear what Julia herself felt at such times. Perhaps she was less in need of expressing her thoughts and feelings, yet her love for her children shows very clearly in her letters. It may be that as *"a good woman"* it was impossible for her to be demonstrative. Rush's own words seem to confirm this possibility: "She fulfilled every duty as wife, mother, and mistress with fidelity and integrity."

12. The Seeds of Slavery

BY THE TIME RUSH MARRIED Julia Stockton in January of 1776, he was in the midst of the typhoon of the American Revolution. It was to buffet him even more violently than most men, for he knew too little about trimming sail in a high wind. It was his habit to sail straight on under full canvas. He once said, "Prudence is a rascally virtue." His unsigned letters, and the pen names and anonymity he sometimes assumed during the Revolution, were a kind of prudent camouflage, but then camouflage has always been standard combat procedure.

His first published imprudence was his *Address ... Upon Slave-Keeping*, which appeared in 1772. Its description of a slave market is enough to melt the heart of anyone but a Simon Legree or a plantation owner whose gracious way of life was endangered by an attack on slavery. "It has been reprinted in New York and Boston," he wrote to his Parisian friend Dubourg, "where it has aroused the zeal of a number of ardent and eloquent defenders of justice, liberty, and humanity." It helped to do more than that. "A law," he added, "has been passed which levies a tax from £7 to £14 per head upon Negro slaves; this amounts to an almost total prohibition."

The law failed to endear Rush to large slave owners, who wanted to import more slaves. It also may help to explain why Rush, in 1773, refused an offer of a thousand guineas a year to practice in Charleston, South Carolina, but we must believe that the main reason was the one he gave Dubourg. "I am too attached to my own country," he explained, "this dear province where one owes one's ease only to free and honest toil, to be tempted to exchange it for a country where wealth has been accumulated only by the sweat and blood of Negro slaves." For a man feeling this way it was only natural to help organize the first American anti-slavery society in 1774, and very fitting that many years later he should succeed Franklin as its president.

His anti-slavery activities made him a "political" doctor and unpopular not only among pro-slavery men but among his fellow doctors, who thought he should stick to his doctoring. Of course, his medical colleagues also disliked his Cullenism, and so had two reasons for not referring patients to him. Some of them also disapproved of his anti-British views, and doubtless encouraged wealthy Tories in their boycott of the young maverick.

By 1774, nonetheless, he was able to write that "my success in business has exceeded the expectations with which I left London." His practice increased steadily. By 1775, his income was about £900 a year, a reasonably good income at the time. In July, 1776, he wrote Julia that "I was willing to be poor that my country might be free. The latter, I hope will

be granted, and contrary even to my wishes I find I am growing rich."

This discovery was somewhat illusory, but whether by
reason of "business" success or social charm he had become
socially eligible as early as 1773, though not among the rab-
idly pro-British. At the time the studious and serious young
bachelor disapproved of such popular diversions as horse-
racing, cock-fighting, and alcoholic socializing in taverns, but
he had no objection, in principle, to dancing, table games,
music recitals, hunting, fishing, swimming, and skating. He
was just too busy for much social life or for sports. But as
revolutionary activity increased in Philadelphia, he was often
forced, as John Adams complained to his wife Abigail, to
"feast upon ten thousand delicacies and sit drinking Madeira,
Claret and Burgundy till six or seven, and then go home
fatigued to death with business, company, and care."

Because of his education, reading and experience abroad
Rush, though not wealthy, had many friends in the upper
class — among merchants, bankers, government officials and
professionals. Their society, however, was not everything he
could have wished. In 1774, he wrote to his Virginia friend
Arthur Lee, then in London, about an "oration" he had
delivered "on the natural history of medicine among the Indians," which he hoped might find a publisher in England.
But, he went on, "you must apologize for the author by plead-
ing his many disadvantages from the want of leisure, books,
and literary company." Philadelphia, he had found, was not
up to the cultural level of Edinburgh, London and Paris.

But Philadelphia did have its intellectual salons. Unlike
those in Paris, they were normally attended by men only.
The rule had at least one exception, however. In the magnificent house of Dr. Thomas Graeme, where Rush had
entrée, the salons were attended by both men and women.
They discussed politics, science, art and literature. Often the

guests included distinguished foreigners, as well as members of the American elite from other colonies. The hostess was the talented Elizabeth Graeme, daughter of the widowed doctor. She became one of Rush's lifelong friends, and he named a daughter after her.

A much-discussed topic at all salons as in every tavern was that of American grievances against the mother country. Like France and other imperial European powers, Britain had always believed that her colonies existed only for her own benefit. Under the Navigation Acts, trade between Britain and her American colonies was a highly profitable one-way street.

No colony could deal directly with any other country. Everything going from or coming into the colonies had to pass through the hands of British merchants in England. They bought American products and sold them at a profit in Europe. They bought European products and sold them at a profit in America. The British merchants, then, took an unnecessary middleman's profit, which had to be added onto a reasonable selling price at both ends of the trade shuttle. Making the selling price even higher was the charge for carrying products across the Atlantic, a charge that went mainly into British shipowners' pockets, though there were colonial shipowners, too. American agricultural products, moreover, could be sold in England only after the shipper, an American, paid a tax on every bushel, which meant revenue for the Crown. This tax was also passed on to the ultimate buyer.

Nor is this the end of the story. Britain, wishing to develop her own manufactures, prohibited manufacturing in the colonies, except for home spinning and weaving and other minor handicrafts. Raw materials had to go to England for manufacture. Manufactured products were then sold back to the colonists at handsome prices.

The whole system was calculated to eliminate competition and competitive pricing from any source, European or American, and to increase the wealth and glory of England.

In early colonial times trade was small and unimportant, so that the Navigation Acts were not enforced. But at about the time the French and Indian War ended in 1763, things changed. George III came to the throne, and Britain began to crack down. The Americans retaliated by refusing to import British goods. Trade came virtually to a standstill, and the colonists began to get the notion that each colony should make its own laws. The British would have none of this. They even decided that the Americans ought to help foot the bill for the recent French and Indian War. The result was a batch of new tax laws, among them the hated Stamp Act of 1765, placing a tax on all legal papers.

The British were dumbfounded by the result. In several colonies the Sons of Liberty sprang up to fight the tax. The cry "No taxation without representation" was loud in the land. Even British merchants, feeling the pinch of the American boycott, found the tax unwise and unprofitable. The boycott had stifled trade and, among other things, had made it impossible for southern planters to pay their large debts to their British creditors. To make things worse, British and Irish radicals agreed that "Taxation without Representation is Tyranny."

In 1766, the year Rush went to Edinburgh, the Stamp Act was repealed, and for a short time there was peace. But in the same year Parliament asserted its right to make any colonial laws it pleased and, in 1767, through the Townshend Laws, imposed duties on glass, lead, paints, paper and tea.

An American Board of Commissioners of the customs at Boston was created which was directly responsible to the British Treasury Board. Its authority to collect the duties allowed the use of "writs of assistance," which meant that the Commission could invade private warehouses and homes in search of contraband goods. The moneys collected were used by the British to defray the cost of searchers, officers and staffs, so that the governors did not have to appeal to the assemblies of the colonies for funds.

Coincidentally, somewhat later in the same year, the New York Legislature was ordered under suspension by Townshend, although this was not part of the Acts. This was done as a reprisal for nonconformist actions of several cities — the refusal to quarter the British troops as provided by the Quartering Act of 1765.

The short peace that had followed the repeal of the Stamp Act now came to an end. Americans, feeling the threat to the principle of self-government, again refused to import British goods. The Sons of Liberty — "Liberty Boys" — of Boston came alive again. They demonstrated in the streets, hounded customs officials, and tarred and feathered British informers. The next year, 1768, British regular troops arrived in Boston to enforce peace and compliance.

For the next two years no very dramatic violence occurred, but in 1770 the troops fired into a Boston street crowd, killing five workingmen, among them the fugitive slave Crispus Attucks. The affair came to be known as the Boston Massacre. Merchants, who wished to see peace and trade restored, now organized to combat what they called "the unbridled Spirit of Mob Violence," though in the Massacre the violence had come from the troops.

The merchants were rewarded by the repeal of all the Townshend duties, except the three pence tax on tea. In itself the tax was not burdensome. Most of the tea being drunk in the colonies was smuggled Dutch tea, anyway. But the tax was symbolic. The Boston Liberty Boys and others saw in it the threat of continued British arbitrary rule, and the tax was still taxation without representation. It was still tyranny.

This was bad enough, but Parliament promptly made things worse. Although the British East India Company had a virtual monopoly of the legal colonial tea trade, through mismanagement, it was near bankruptcy. Parliament leaped to its rescue. Normally, tea imported into England for re-shipment to the colonies was taxed, which meant that the Company added the tax to the colonial selling price. If it were relieved of this tax, the Company could sell the tea cheaper in the colonies, cheaper even than in England. It could also undersell the Dutch tea smugglers. Surely the Americans would not object to this.

Unfortunately, there was a huge stock of unsold Dutch tea, as well as legal tea bought at higher prices, in American hands. If the cheaper Company tea were allowed to compete, Americans already holding tea would take a big loss. American consumers had nothing to lose, but again there was a principle at stake, the principle of self-government opposed to the threatened Company monopoly and the Townshend tax. The Boston populace, therefore, supported the stand of the merchants and traders against the landing of the tea.

Rush saw eye to eye with the Bostonians. On October 10, 1773, he wrote to a Massachusetts clergyman that "We are preparing here to oppose the landing of the East India tea" — that is, from the ship *Polly*, which was headed for Philadelphia. On October 20 he published a letter, *On Patriotism,* addressed *To His Fellow Countrymen* and prudently signed "Hamden." In it he wrote that "Patriotism is as much a virtue, and is as necessary for the support of societies as natural affection is for the support of families... You have heard of the machinations of the enemies of our country to enslave us by means of the East-India Company. By the last account from Britain we are informed that vessels were freighted to bring over a quantity of tea taxed with a duty [that is, the Townshend duty] to raise revenue from America.

Should it be landed, it is to be feared it will find its way
amongst us. Then farewell American Liberty! . . . Let us with
ONE heart oppose the landing of it. The baneful chests . . .
contain something worse than death — the seeds of *SLAV-
ERY.*"

Early in December, 1773, several tea ships arrived in Boston. Encouraged by Rush's letter *On Patriotism* and by other
publications and speeches, the Bostonians pledged their
"lives and fortunes" against allowing the ships' cargo to be
landed. A Liberty Boy leader suggested dumping the tea
into the harbor, and on December 16 a number of Bostonians
disguised as Indians held the Boston Tea Party. All the tea
went overboard into the bay. Eleven days later — chiefly
through the efforts of Rush and his friends William Bradford (Thomas' father) and Thomas Mifflin — the ship *Polly,*
carrying the tea, was turned back from Philadelphia. The
same thing happened to a ship in New York.

British trade policy had once more proved impracticable in
America. The plan to rescue the East India Company from
bankruptcy was like Will Rogers' plan to eliminate the German submarine menace in World War I. "All you have to
do," he said, "is to heat the Atlantic to 212 degrees. Then
the subs will have to come up and we can pick them off. Of
course, somebody's going to want to know how to heat up the
ocean. I'm not worrying about that. That's just a detail, and
I'm a policy maker."

The detail that British policy makers did not know how
to handle was how to pacify the colonies. Their next move
succeeded beautifully in inflaming them even more. This
was the passage of the Boston Port Bill, effective June 1, 1774,
which closed Boston harbor to trade until the dumped tea
had been paid for.

Other "Intolerable Acts" followed. British agents charged
with offenses in Massachusetts, a new law said, could be tried

in other colonies or in England. Bostonians were to quarter British troops in their homes. The Royal governor's powers were extended. The policy makers took the view of Dr. Samuel Johnson, that Americans "ought to be thankful for anything we allow them short of hanging." The Bostonians, then, should be thankful for merely being starved to death. The other colonies should be thankful for being given the chance to profit from Boston's horrible example.

Most Americans chose not to be thankful. Northern manufacturers and shippers, in direct competition with Britain, were the first to see the need for united action against the strangulation of Boston. Many southerners, though not at all in competition, were not long behindhand. By 1774, because of special laws directed against the South, they could see that what had happened in Massachusetts could happen in the Carolinas or Virginia. There was, therefore, a need to assert the "common rights" of all the colonies.

"I am not only a Virginian," cried Patrick Henry, "I am also an American." The Virginians, who gathered at Williamsburg's Bruton Parish Church in "fasting, humiliation and prayer," were just as outraged at Boston's treatment as he was. Carolinians gave substantial evidence of their sympathy by sending provisions to Boston.

Of course, Pennsylvania — with such leaders as Franklin, Bradford, Mifflin and Rush — did not hesitate for a moment. Philadelphians muffled their church bells and flew their flags at half-staff. *E Pluribus Unum,* "from many, one," became the watchword. Franklin, with his gift for memorable statement, best summed up the colonial choice: "We shall hang together or hang separately." Sam Adams, John Adams, and John Hancock of Massachusetts agreed with him. So did George Washington, Thomas Jefferson, and Patrick Henry of Virginia. And so did Benjamin Rush.

Nevertheless, there were many who thought that reconciliation of imperial and colonial differences was still possible. The view was commonest in the South. But even in the North, many a heart as stout as Sam Adams's found it expedient to seem to agree — in part. The times were dangerous and Britain was the strongest power on earth. Even Rush, who deemed prudence "a rascally virtue," found it expedient, in such times, to be prudent on occasion.

 ## 13. Rebels and Gunpowder

MORE THAN A YEAR BEFORE the Boston Tea Party, in 1773, and the Intolerable Acts that followed, Massachusetts' patriots had seen the need for an "intelligence" system. The towns of the Bay Colony had to be kept informed and, to fill the need, the Boston Sons of Liberty — led by Sam Adams, and assisted by such men as the artisan Paul Revere — organized the Boston Committee of Correspondence. As affairs with Britain grew worse in 1773 and 1774, similar committees sprang up in other colonies, north and south.

Correspondence, however, was slow, and even at best it was not an adequate substitute for face-to-face exchange of information and views. It became clear that a general assembly of representatives of all thirteen colonies was needed. The result was the convening of the First Continental Congress in Philadelphia on September 5, 1774.

The fifty-five delegates represented every colony and all classes. Some were conservative southern plantation owners, urging the "reasonableness of Englishmen." Some were moderates, like John Dickinson of Pennsylvania. Some were radicals, like Sam Adams of Massachusetts and Patrick Henry of Virginia. There were philosophers, doctors, lawyers, politicians, tradesmen, farmers, hunters. The important thing they had in common was a hatred of British oppression.

Benjamin Rush was on the committee selected to greet the New England delegates at Frankford, on the outskirts of Philadelphia, and to escort them into the city. It was a delicate mission. Many rich Philadelphians considered the Bostonians altogether too democratic and too much in favor of rebellion. The greeting committee was to apprise the New Englanders of this, and urge them to walk and to talk softly.

Rush says that he "rode back into town in the same carriage with John Adams ... He asked me many questions relative to the state of public opinion upon politicks, and the characters of the most active citizens on both sides of the controversy." Exactly how Rush answered the questions he does not tell us. During the ride, however, and later, when both John and Samuel Adams lived in Rush's house, he seems to have talked more — and more imprudently — about his radical acquaintances than John Adams had a taste for. At any rate, Adams did not get a good first impression of the young doctor as a man of politics. One of Adams' "Diary" entries said that Rush was "an elegant, ingenious body ... too much of a talker to be a deep thinker; elegant, not great." He was to change his opinion of the young doctor before long, and the friendship between the two men was to become one of the most lasting in Rush's life, despite many continuing differences.

"I waited upon nearly all the members of this first Congress," Rush wrote in his *Autobiography*, "and entertained most of them at my table." Notable among his guests were the Virginia delegates George Washington, Richard Henry Lee — brother-in-law of Rush's dearest enemy, Dr. Shippen — and Patrick Henry, whom Rush inoculated for smallpox.

During the First Continental Congress there was much socializing. John Adams was not the only one to complain about it. One event was a dinner at Dr. Thomas Mifflin's, where, Rush reports, he "spent a long evening...in company with George Washington, the two Adamses, Charles Lee...and several other gentlemen who acted a conspicuous part in the American Revolution." Lee later became a general, but at this time he was not too sympathetic toward rebellion-minded Bostonians. John Adams, nevertheless, according to Rush, "said he had no expectation of a redress of grievances and a reconciliation with Great Britain, and as proof of this belief, he gave a toast "Cash and Gunpowder to the Yankies,'" because he expected "the war would begin among the New Englandmen."

The first Congress managed to agree well enough to adopt a Declaration of Rights and Grievances. It also agreed not to import British goods after December 1, 1774. The delegates were pledged to form local committees in every town, city and county to enforce the agreement and to report violations.

Early in the evening of the day of adjournment, Washington dined with Rush at his home. From there the two men went to the City Tavern, where the visiting delegates entertained their Philadelphia hosts at supper. "The company was large," Rush wrote, "and the conversation animated by the most fervid patriotism." Governor Samuel Ward of Rhode Island raised his glass in a toast: "May the fire which has been recently kindled upon the altar of liberty in America, enlighten all the nations of the world into a knowledge of their rights."

The devotion, unselfishness and patriotic fervor, displayed

at the Congress, encouraged and inspired Rush. He committed himself irretrievably to the cause of freedom, and under a variety of pen names shot off letter after letter to the press. By this means, he said, "an impression . . . in favor of liberty was made upon the minds of its friends and enemies."

THE provincial assemblies at once ratified the decisions of the Congress and set up Committees of Inspection in nearly every town, of the now united colonies, to enforce the new non-importation agreement. Shopkeepers who violated it were hunted down, their British goods dumped into the streets, and the shopkeepers themselves often tarred and feathered. The boycott was effective. In Philadelphia alone imports from Great Britain fell from more than £625,000 in 1774 to £1,366 in 1775. Throughout the colonies, British trade declined by 93 per cent. Once more British policy had proved impracticable in America.

British manufacturers petitioned Parliament to repeal the Acts that had proved so unworkable and unprofitable. In the House of Commons, Edmund Burke eloquently urged abandonment of the course that, he feared, was leading to war. "In order that Parliament may be free," he said, "it is necessary that the colonies be free." But the neck of George III remained stubbornly stiff. "The die is cast," he said, "the colonists must either submit or triumph."

The colonists preferred the second of the King's alternatives, and Philadelphians, led by Rush, worked out a plan that promised to make "triumph" more than a mere patriotic ambition. They formed a joint stock company for the manufacture of cloth, the principal import from Britain, and called it the United Company for Promoting American Manufactures. Less than a month after its first general meeting, the Company's stockholders elected Rush president.

On that day — March 16, 1775 — the new president spoke

on the need for and purposes of the organization. Since British woolen, cotton and linen cloth was under boycott, similar cloth had to be made in America, which would render the boycott all the more effective. Many families were already spinning their own wool and flax, but only factories could fill the gap made by the embargo and bring the British policy makers to their senses.

Rush urged improvement in the breeding of sheep so that there might be enough wool to clothe everyone. And cotton from the South and from the West Indies, he said, could be processed right in Philadelphia and sold at a lower price than British cotton goods. Philadelphia and Pennsylvania would flourish, and trade with the South would strengthen its ties with the North. If only half the citizens of Pennsylvania used their average clothing expenditure of five pounds a year to buy domestic instead of British cloth, the province would keep £ 250,000 at home, employ very many more workers, encourage immigration from Europe, and in time make America self-sufficient. The stockholders recognized Rush's plan as not only rational but practicable, and endorsed it enthusiastically.

One of the early fruits of the plan was the United Company's introduction of the first spinning jenny into the colonies. Soon, hundreds of women were employed in making cloth. The American textile industry had been launched. Its objective, in addition to making money, was to free the colonies from subjection to British industry. The Rush plan caught on in other parts of the country, notably in New England under the sponsorship of the Sons of Liberty.

To his role as propagandist, medical and political, Rush had now added the role of industrial organizer and promoter. In doing so, he had added another "first" to his growing list, that of first American industrial textile executive.

MEANWHILE in Massachusetts, as John Adams had prophesied, events were rapidly coming to a climax. The Massachusetts Assembly was preparing to resist enforcement of the repressive Acts of Parliament. Under the Assembly's direction munitions were being stored, civilians organized into military companies, and officers commissioned to drill them. Paul Revere — a leader of the people along with Sam Adams — created an espionage system to keep track of British plans and troop movements.

Exactly one month after Rush had become president of the United Company in Philadelphia, Revere rode from Boston to Lexington to warn Sam Adams and the lawyer John Hancock that the British General Gage intended to arrest them. This was April 16, 1775. Two days later he once more rode to Lexington, arriving at midnight, this time to conduct Adams and Hancock to safer quarters and on the way to warn the countryside that British troops were marching from Boston. The next day, April 19, the British, some 700 strong, reached Lexington, where perhaps seventy Minute Men blocked their way. Afterward no one knew for sure who fired first, but no matter, it was the "shot heard round the world." The American Revolution had begun.

After a skirmish, the British moved for seven miles on to Concord and encountered many more shots at that little bridge over a "dark stream." The British soon had enough of the "embattled farmers" and turned back toward Boston. As they retreated, marksmen shot at them from behind every rock, wall, bush, tree and barn. The British lost about a third of their force, and some one hundred Americans died.

The news that home-grown militiamen had walloped the redcoats traveled fast. Pledges of support came from all over the Bay Colony. It was not yet clear to most Americans that the die was cast, but it was clear to Rush. "The Battle of Lexington," he wrote, "gave a new tone to my feelings, and I now resolved to bear my share of the duties and burdens of the approaching Revolution. I considered the seperation of the colonies from Great Britain as inevitable. The first gun that was fired at an American cut the cord that had tied the two countries together. It was the signal for the commencement of our independance and from this time all my publications were calculated to prepare the public mind to adopt that important and necesssary measure."

THREE weeks after Lexington and Concord, the Second Continental Congress convened at the State House in Philadelphia in an atmosphere of tension. Such men as Franklin, the two Adamses, Thomas Jefferson, Patrick Henry and Benjamin Rush were now convinced that the time for mere spoken and written protest was over. It was time for open resistance and a demand for complete independence.

How unsure others were is clear from Rush's report of something that befell John Adams during the Second Congress. "The independance of the United States was first brought before the public mind in 1775 by a letter from him [Adams] to one of his friends in Massachusetts that was intercepted and published in Boston, in which he expressed a wish for that measure. It exposed him to the execrations of all the prudent and moderate people in America, insomuch that he was treated with neglect by many of his old friends."

But the revolutionary tide was now too strong to be stemmed by the "prudent and moderate." On June 15, 1775 — two days before the Battle of Bunker Hill — the Congress, on the motion of John Adams, selected George Washington to command the Continental Army. George III proclaimed a state of "open and avowed rebellion" in the colonies. In the King's eyes, as in the eyes of prudent and moderate Americans, the struggle was still only a rebellion — the colonies were still colonies.

Franklin, Jefferson, Rush and some dozen other men, who

honored Washington with a dinner at Mullen's Tavern shortly after his appointment, were not of the prudent and moderate breed. "The first toast that was given after dinner," Rush reported, "was 'The Commander in Chief of the American Armies.' General Washington rose from his seat, and with some confusion thanked the company for the honor they did him. The whole company rose, and drank the toast standing."

Washington's "confusion" was not mock modesty. "About this time," Rush says, "I saw Patrick Henry at his lodgings, who told me that General Washington had been with him, and informed him that he was unequal to the station in which his country had placed him, and then added with tears in his eyes 'Remember, Mr. Henry, what I now tell you: From the day I enter upon the command of the American armies, I date my fall, and the ruin of my reputation.'"

On July 3, 1775, under a great elm tree in Cambridge, across the Charles River from Boston, Washington assumed actual command. It is not given to every general to have his reputation "ruined" so gloriously. By October Rush was moved to write to a friend that "General Washington has astonished his most intimate friends with a display of the most wonderful talents for the government of an army." Rush's view of Washington's talents was to change later, but in these early days he was one of the general's most ardent admirers.

BACK in 1774, John Adams had called for "Cash and Gunpowder to the Yankies." Cash could be collected from patriots who were not too prudent and moderate, but saltpeter (potassium nitrate), a necessary ingredient of gunpowder, could not be collected in sufficient quantity from present stocks. It had to be manufactured. Who knew how to do it? The answer was Dr. Benjamin Rush, authority on the chemistry of saltpeter. His "Process of Making Salt-Petre" was first published in the *Pennsylvania Journal* in January, 1775. Revised and enlarged, it was republished in June in the *Pennsylvania Magazine,* edited by Thomas Paine. Four months later Rush wrote to an old schoolmate that "We expect to make enough in a year to supply gunpowder for an American fleet as well as an army." The letter somehow fell into British hands. Rush was now in the same boat as John Adams after his letter had been intercepted. Both were now on the list of "most wanted" traitors to Mother England.

Pennsylvania had decided to follow the lead of Massachusetts and take steps toward local protection. The Committee of Public Safety, under the leadership of Franklin, began building a fleet of gunboats to guard the Delaware River, the entrance to Philadelphia from the sea. Vessels, propelled by oars, were fitted with howitzers and muskets, probably primed with some of Rush's first output of gunpowder. The gunpowder expert was also made surgeon of the fleet, a position he held for ten months. His training in military medicine, under Sir John Pringle in London, was beginning to pay off. It was to pay off even more later on — and get him into one of the biggest battles of his life.

 ## 14. Founding Father

AT THE BEGINNING OF 1775, the idea of a war for independence was present in relatively few minds. An overwhelming majority of Americans, however, had had enough of British tyranny. The Second Continental Congress, then, was only carrying out the will of the majority when it began coordinating national activities, declared that a state of war existed, and placed General Washington at the head of a national army.

But it was one thing to agree that a state of war existed and another thing to agree on what kind of war it was. Was it a war merely to force a redress of grievances? Was it only a rebellion, as King George believed? Or what?

Tories — rich landlords, that is, big merchants, Crown officials, well-heeled professional men — agreed with the King. The vast majority of Americans — Whigs, Patriots — were of another mind. Or, rather, of several minds.

The Tories, a small minority, were all well fixed, well born, or well placed and, generally speaking, well educated. The Patriots were a bafflingly mixed mass. They were merchants and tradesmen, doctors and lawyers, mechanics and workers, artisans, small farmers, hunters and trappers. They were also aristocratic planters like Washington, Madison and Jefferson of Virginia. They were frontiersmen west of the Alleghenies. They were rich and learned men as well as poor and ignorant men.

The Tories, like-minded and of similar interests, found it easy to agree. The Patriots, being of many minds and many interests, had diverse points of view.

The heart of their differences lay in the special interests of groups, classes and regions. Even under the old trade restrictions, many Northern merchants and tradesmen prospered. If they followed the lead of the New England radicals like Sam Adams and his Liberty Boys, they might regret it. If defeated in war, they might face treason charges, might lose all their trade and all their property. Then again, if the Patriots fought and won without their help, it was likely that they would lose their prestige and their traditional share of control over government. "Mob rule" would take over. The aristocratic planters of Virginia and Carolina were equally opposed to "mob rule." Religious factionalism also divided the Patriots. Church of England people — the "best" people, — were revolted at the thought of unscrubbed Presbyterians lording it over them, if the British and the Tories lost the war.

But, after Lexington and Concord and Bunker Hill, after British naval vessels burned the town of Falmouth, Maine, after the King rejected conciliation, after Parliament passed an Act to prohibit all trade with the colonies — after all these events of 1775, the idea of a war that would put an end to British oppression gained ground.

Now the Northern merchants got their hackles up. Now the

old British-oriented colonial governments came under pressure. When the news of Lexington and Concord reached New York, for example, a citizens' Voluntary Corps took over the city government. In other colonies, popular congresses first issued remonstrances, then seized government control. By the end of 1775, these congresses controlled ten of the thirteen colonies. In only a few more months they controlled all thirteen.

Despite a well-bred suspicion of the "lower classes," the Southern planters, also, had reasons for going along with the war movement. They had long been deeply in debt to British creditors. For some time, many of them, especially in Virginia, had been trying to raise money to pay the debts, or at least the interest on them, by speculating in land in the Cumberland and Ohio valleys west of the Alleghenies. The Quebec Act which guaranteed the French freedom of worship and property rights — and the new Crown regulations of 1774, had shattered that dream by closing much of the Western land to speculation.

The Southern speculators now faced ruin, and, by 1775, many of them were ready to join up for the war. Victory could mean an open road to riches in the now-forbidden West.

Of course, the bona fide Western frontiersmen — who were there chiefly to clear and cultivate the land — also stood to gain from a successful war. They would then be able to settle where the land was richest, regardless of royal whim and British greed.

The fact was that there were many on both sides of the argument over the desirability of war, who acted out of self-interest. But there was a more important fact: the great majority of the American people loved liberty and justice for their own sake. It was chiefly this majority who could most easily be won over to a war for independence. It was only the die-hard Tories who were completely hopeless.

On that fall evening when Tom Paine left Dr. Rush's home, he walked to his barren little room and set to work on the pamphlet that the two had discussed. They had agreed to call it *Common Sense* because it was to contain nothing but common sense and would, they hoped, convince everyone with common sense that the war should become a war for independence. But writing common sense that would *seem* like common sense to widely scattered Americans of so many sorts and conditions was not easy.

Paine wrote and rewrote what he had written several times trying to make every phrase, every clause, every sentence as sharp as a dagger-point. When he felt that a chapter was as clear and convincing as he could make it, he would take it into the coffee houses and taverns and read it to anyone who would listen. Then, after further rewriting, he would read the chapter to Dr. Rush and perhaps rewrite once more.

Finally the pamphlet was finished. And published, after it had been shown to a few important friends of independence, who urged its publication.

It was now December, 1775, and Paine and Rush saw each other once more by the light of the candles on the doctor's table. The small manuscript lay on the table between them. For some time they just looked at it soberly and in silence. At last Paine looked up at his friend and grinned.

"Well, doctor," he said, "there's our baby. Do you think it will live?"

Rush looked up. "I'm sure it will," he said. "It will live to make a big noise in the world. You have done a magnificent piece of writing, far better than I could have done."

"Thank you, sir, but who's to publish it? It will be dangerous work."

"Yes, it will," Rush admitted, "but somewhere I promise to find a publisher."

Paine rose from his chair. "I must leave you, then," he said. "My job is done."

Rush, too, rose to his feet. "Your job, yes," he said, "but not your reward. I will see that the publisher is fair to you."

Paine's voice came harsh over the candles. "You will do nothing of the sort, sir! I am not a petty hireling in the cause of liberty! I am not a mercenary soldier!"

For a moment neither spoke. The candlelight played faintly on their faces . . . . At length Rush spoke.

"So be it," he said.

"So be it," Paine answered.

Their hands clasped over the table. Paine grinned again. "I will soon join General Washington's army," he said. "If this little book is published and the author becomes known, I will not long be welcome among our Tory friends here in Philadelphia."

"Nor I," Rush said. "They may suspect I am the author. *Common Sense* sounds like me."

Paine laughed. "It does indeed."

At the Front Street door they shook hands. Rush turned back into the house, closed the door, and walked into his study. He took a book from a shelf, sat down at the table, and began reading *De l'Esprit des Lois,* the spirit of laws. He was reading up on constitutions. Pennsylvania would soon be needing one.

Paine walked away along Front Street. His name was still not widely known, but soon it would be, and would remain forever bright in the annals of the struggle for independence.

RUSH kept his promise. He did find a publisher for *Common Sense.* The publisher was Robert Bell, a man of courage. The pamphlet that shook the colonies awake appeared anonymously on January 10, 1776, while Washington was besieging Boston. The little book became famous overnight, and by the end of spring more than 120,000 copies had been sold. It has even been estimated that altogether some 500,000 of the three million Americans bought it. *"Common Sense,"* Rush wrote, "was read by public men, repeated in clubs, spouted in schools, and in one instance, delivered from the pulpit instead of a sermon by a clergyman in Connecticut. Several pamphlets were written against it, but they fell dead from the press. The controversy was carried into the newspapers, in which I bore a busy part."

Common Sense was no humble remonstrance, no meek petition to the King. It breathed fire and brimstone. It singed the beards of kings everywhere and in every time. "The heathens," it said, "paid divine honors to their deceased kings, and the Christian world has improved on the plan by doing the same to their living ones ... Of more worth is one honest man to society, and in the sight of God, than all the crowned ruffians that ever lived."

About "the excellent British constitution," Paine said: "It is the most complicated, irrational, and ridiculous contrivance ever devised to govern enlightened men." It did not protect the English people from oppression any more than it had protected her colonies. If Britain had protected the colonies, it was for her own profit, not for their good. " 'But Britain is the parent country,' say some. Then the more shame upon her conduct. Even brutes do not devour their young, nor savages make war upon their families."

Reconciliation with such a cannibalistic mother, then, Paine concluded, was out of the question. She would only devour America at her leisure and get it embroiled in all her European quarrels to boot. No, the colonies should declare themselves free and independent states and establish in America a haven for the oppressed peoples of the world. "Let the names of Whig and Tory be extinct; and let none other be heard among us, than those of *a good citizen; an open and resolute friend;* and *a virtuous supporter* of the *RIGHTS OF MANKIND,* and of the *FREE AND INDEPENDENT STATES OF AMERICA.*"

Some three months after its publication, Washington wrote: "My countrymen, I know, from their form of government and steady attachment heretofore to royalty will come reluctantly into the idea of independence, but time and persecution bring many wonderful things to pass; ... I find Common Sense is working a powerful change in the minds of men."

Who had manufactured this little but mighty bomb, men wondered. Some of Rush's friends, including John Adams and Charles Lee, were sure Rush had.

As the weeks and months of 1776 advanced toward an open declaration of independence, for which *Common Sense* was the first clear and most persuasive call, Rush became even busier. As a Pennsylvanian, he wished to make sure that his native province aligned itself with the cause of common sense and independence. There was reason to believe that it would not — at least if the Pennsylvania Assembly had its way.

The Assembly, meeting in one part of the State House while the Continental Congress of 1776 convened in another, was controlled by Tories. Their views were the most conservative of the small minority of Pennsylvanians who could meet the property qualifications for voting and holding office. The Tory Assembly, then, did not speak for the great majority in opposing separation from Britain. But in those warm days of May, the revolutionary sentiments of the mass of Philadelphians kept pace with the rising thermometer readings. People opposed to the war were becoming extremely unpopular.

With his makeshift army General Washington had joined battle with the British near Boston. He needed food and other supplies, and the people of Philadelphia — supply center and seat of the Congress — would tolerate no hoarding by merchants, no Royalist nonsense. Bloody noses and broken bones might be followed by worse if the hoarding and traitorous activities continued.

A clear case of treachery, ordinary Philadelphians felt, was the behavior of the Tory-dominated Pennsylvania Assembly. On May 20, a crowd of over six thousand gathered in the State House yard and demanded that the Assembly be liquidated. It was agreed that a provincial conference should be held a month later to work out details for the election of a truly representative Assembly, which meant one that would support independence. Rush, as an elected member of the forthcoming conference, was in the thick of things.

How necessary it was to get rid of the old Assembly soon became clear. On June 7, Richard Henry Lee, speaking for the Virginia delegation in the Continental Congress, presented a resolution for independence. The delegates to the Congress from the Pennsylvania Assembly voted five to one against it, conclusive proof that the Tory Assembly was out of step with the times. The Patriot minority in the Assembly bolted, leaving it without a quorum. The old Assembly was dead.

The provincial conference to which Rush had been elected met in Carpenter's Hall on June 18. It endorsed a new oath of allegiance that omitted all reference to the King. Rush wrote the declaration annulling the old government. He also helped to arrange for a convention that was to write a new constitution for Pennsylvania. Then he went home and continued to study constitution-making. Rush never went into anything without preparation, not if he could help it.

On June 23, Rush moved that the provincial conference draft a statement in favor of American independence. The conference at once made him chairman of the drafting committee. He didn't allow his committee to sleep on the job. The very next day its declaration of principles was submitted and the conference adopted it. The principles anticipated by a few days some of those included by Jefferson in the Declaration of Independence.

On June 25, at the Indian Queen Tavern on Fourth Street, the provincial conference toasted "the free and independent States of America." The conference was unofficial and its toast a few days premature, but in this action Pennsylvania had stood up to be counted. Rush had carried Pennsylvania.

The Continental Congress *declared* independence on July 2 and 3. The formal Declaration was *adopted* on July 4. The only signature that went on it that day was John Hancock's, the president of the Congress. When the fateful document was placed before him on the table, he eagerly seized a quill, dipped it in ink, and wrote his name large and beautiful. Tradition has it that when he had finished, he threw down the quill and said, "There! George ought to be able to see *that* without his glasses!" The George he meant was George III.

The Pennsylvania Constitutional Convention met on July 15, chose Benjamin Franklin as its president, set up a new Council of Safety as a temporary governing body, and began framing a state constitution. The framers — all liberals — wanted the same thing as the western farmers and other common people of Pennsylvania, and, therefore, had their support. The constitution, when finished, extended the franchise and provided for democratic representation, complete religious freedom, and a one-chamber legislature to be elected annually.

The new constitution was among the most advanced of the first state constitutions, but it was not perfect. Rush objected vigorously to one imperfection. He fought against the provision for a one-chamber legislature on the ground that it

The Declaration of Independence

violated the principle of checks and balances necessary to the democratic process.

His criticism was to lose him popularity later on, but in the early stages of the constitutional debate he was still riding the crest of the wave. On July 20, the Convention elected Rush and eight others favoring independence as its delegates to Congress. He was, therefore, in Congress on August 2, the historic moment when all but a few absent members added their signatures to the Declaration of Independence under the large and beautiful "John Hancock" at the top.

By this stroke of well-deserved fortune, "Benjamin Rush" appears on the most precious of American documents. While yet only thirty, he joined the most illustrious company of men in our history — John Hancock, Benjamin Franklin, John Adams, Samuel Adams, Thomas Jefferson, Robert Morris — "financier of the Revolution" — and so on down the line of Founding Fathers. It is a great pity that the names of George Washington, with the fighting heart, and Tom Paine, who "worked a powerful change in the minds of men," could not appear among the eventual fifty-five signers.

These United Colonies Are, and of Right Ought To Be, Free and Independent States

With the publication of these words, no one of common sense could doubt the true nature of the war. Many who had been wavering, including some Quakers, now grew firm. Even some former Tories saw the light. The colonies' new determination bore fruit abroad as well as at home. Europe, and especially France, began to welcome the chance to make things tough for an ancient enemy by giving aid to the enemy's colonies.

The united colonies were making things very difficult as it was. Besides his work on the floor of Congress, Congressman

Rush was active on committees. As the leading explosives expert, he was on a committee to improve the quality of gunpowder. He was chairman of a committee charged with supplying the northern army with provisions and medicine. He was appointed to investigate the conditions of prisoners of war. In the fall of 1776, he became chairman of a committee that was to prepare a report on the army and navy. In his spare time he practiced medicine and tried to be a good husband.

ONE of the knotty problems, facing Rush and the other members of the Congress, concerned the number of representatives each state was to have in the projected American confederation. Most of the country's population lived in the large, wealthy states, including Virginia, but especially in the Northern states with the big cities of Philadelphia, New York and Boston. The small states, like Rhode Island and New Hampshire in the North and Carolina in the South, thought that representation should be by states, regardless of size or population. The large states — which necessarily had to provide most of the soldiers, money and supplies to carry on the war — thought that representation should be based on population.

In the debate on the question Rush, like Franklin, sided with the large states. If representation were by state, he argued logically and eloquently, each state would tend to pull for its own instead of for national interests. Congress would thus splinter into factions, which in time would strangle the freedoms of the people. But if representation were based on population, he said, these freedoms would be protected. But what of the danger of the large states combining against the small ones? This was impossible, he contended, because of the geographical separation of the large states. He made it clear that he was not grinding Pennsylvania's private axe. When he entered the door of Congress, he said, he considered himself "a citizen of America."

As an opponent of slavery, Rush had another thought in mind. If representation were based on the number of free citizens, the Southern states, in order to increase the number, might be encouraged to limit slavery.

Just as he hated slavery, Rush had a healthy fear of the military as a caste. He, therefore, argued that the Congress, not the army, should appoint and promote major military officers. The army, and the officer corps in particular, he maintained, should have its roots in the people. "One of the most powerful and happy commonwealths in the world, Rome," he said, "called her general officers from the plough and paid no regard to rank, service or seniority." His own later experience, in trying to correct serious defects in the Continental Army, doubtless confirmed his belief that the military should be responsible to Congress.

However sound this argument may have been, the fact was that America now had a war on her hands. Rush had helped mightily to steer the war in the right direction. Now he wanted to help to achieve victory. He had been doing highly necessary work in the Congress and on his committees, but he was a doctor, and the army needed doctors badly. It was time to move on again — this time to the battlefield and the army hospitals. His practice and Julia would have to get along without him for a while.

15. Baptism of Fire

GENERAL WASHINGTON TOOK HIS ARMY from Boston to face the British on Long Island in midsummer 1776. From then until a few days before the end of the year he had a bad time of it. Outnumbered and outequipped, he could do little but skillfully supervise what was mainly a long, bitter, and painful American retreat. On August 29, to escape a trap set for him by General Howe, he crossed the East River to Manhattan Island. After a victory at the Battle of Harlem Heights, to escape another of Howe's traps he retreated north to White Plains, where he got somewhat the worst of it in another fight.

Washington feared that Howe intended to cross the Hudson River to New Jersey and March south on Philadelphia, the colonial capital. He himself, therefore, crossed the river with about half his army. The other half, under Rush's friend General Charles Lee — a former British army officer — had orders to follow, but he delayed. When he did cross he himself was ignominiously captured, though his troops finally joined Washington's, and the long retreat southward through New Jersey began.

Among the hungry and tattered troops was Tom "Common Sense" Paine, who moved, though on foot, with Washington's staff. Through the long Jersey miles he disputed the principles of the Revolution with a nineteen-year-old staff captain of artillery named Alexander Hamilton. When he was not disputing with the "brilliant boy" or not too hungry and cold, he scribbled, using a drumhead as a desk. He scribbled all the way down New Jersey and across the Delaware into Pennsylvania. By the time the army went into camp there, he had finished his first *Crisis* paper. At headquarters he waited expectantly in front of Washington's table as the general slowly read the paper. When he had finished, Washington handed the weather-beaten manuscript across the table to the author.

"Mr. Paine — " he said, and paused, his eyes on Paine's belt buckle.

"Yes, General?" Paine said, wondering if he had forgotten to polish the buckle.

"Mr. Paine, your *Common Sense* worked wonders. Your *Crisis,* I hope, will work another." He turned to an orderly. "Get Mr. Paine a good horse, and be quick about it!"

The orderly saluted and left the room on the double. Washington looked up into Paine's shining eyes.

"You are to ride to Philadelphia at once and get this paper printed," he said. "I understand your friend Dr. Rush did not go to Baltimore with the Congress. If you need help, I'm sure he will give it. But in any case get this printed at once and send me as many copies as you can spare. I shall need them."

"Yes, General," Paine said, and saluted.

"Godspeed!"

"Good luck to you, sir. You will get your copies by the fastest horse in the city."

Five minutes later Paine was on his way to Philadelphia.

LATE in August, 1776, the Congress, fearing that General Washington could not stop the British advance on Philadelphia, had moved to Baltimore. The departure was the signal for a general exodus of frightened Philadelphians. Congressman Rush remained in Philadelphia where he thought he could be of more use than in Baltimore.

Julia had been living with her parents at Morven, in Princeton, since the spring. By late 1776, she was expecting her first child, and Rush had sent her to live with his cousin Elihu Hall in Cecil County, Maryland. Meanwhile Rush closed their house in the city and moved in with a friend, taking along some of his furniture and books. When the British finally did occupy Philadelphia, in September, 1777, General Howe made this friend's house his headquarters. He used one of Rush's mahogany tables as a desk and marred it with ink spots. After all, it was a rebel's table, and Howe was a British aristocrat.

Rush's resolve to remain in the city stemmed from his general decision to "stand or fall" with his country. The Pennsylvania militia, under General Cadwalader, had gone to Bristol, Pennsylvania, to reinforce Washington's army and help prevent the capture of Philadelphia. Rush joined the militia there and volunteered to supervise its medical section.

On his thirty-first birthday — Christmas Eve, 1776 — he visited General Washington at his headquarters, ten miles above Bristol and four miles from the Delaware River. Joseph Reed — then a colonel in the militia, later Adjutant General of the Continental Army — was Rush's companion on the trip. Reed made the miles long with his gloomy view of the military prospects. After their arrival Rush spent an hour with Washington. The General was also depressed.

"You have seen my army, Dr. Rush," he said. "The men are ragged, cold, ill-fed, sick, and discouraged. They are in no condition or mood to fight, poor fellows. They are sick for the comforts and joys of home, and who can blame them?"

"My heart goes out to them, sir," Rush said, "and to you. Things are bad, but I can assure you the Congress will support you in every way it can."

Washington was grim. "Many of my men are likely to go home when their enlistment terms are over, Doctor. Can the Congress turn a summer soldier, a sunshine patriot, into a winter fighting man, into a snow, sleet, and chilblain patriot?"

Rush smiled without mirth. "It is a good question, General, and well phrased."

Washington put his hand on a big, heavy, paper parcel on the table, quite evidently the wrappings of some printed matter. "The phrasing is inspired, Doctor — inspired by a winter soldier, Thomas Paine. It arrived yesterday in this parcel."

"Is old 'Common Sense' back at it again, sir?" Rush asked, beaming at the parcel.

"You didn't see him in Philadelphia, then?"

"No, sir, but I wish I had."

"Well, no matter, he got it printed, and if I am not mistaken, it will make winter soldiers of us all."

While they were talking, Washington had been writing on several small pieces of paper. One piece now fell to the floor. Rush picked it up and put it back on the table. On it were the words "Victory or Death."

The next day — Christmas day — General Cadwalader, under orders from Washington, moved his Pennsylvania militia to Dunk's ferry near Bristol, Pennsylvania. Dr. Rush, head of the medical section, went along. When the militiamen reached the Delaware River, their officers drew them up along the bank, facing a long row of small boats. Great islands of floating ice choked the river. A heavy, wet snow was falling, mixed with freezing sleet. The men, soaked through and with chattering teeth, stared at the boats, then at the islands of ice, then at each other, and shook their heads.

They knew why they were there. They were to cross to the other side and attack the Hessians in the snug Jersey villages. It was a right good plan. The Hessians, full of Christmas dinner and drunk as dukes, would make the fight strictly no contest. But — boats could not cross through all that ice. General Cadwalader agreed. He ordered the militia back to Bristol. Dr. Rush, disappointed, could only go along.

At dusk of the same day General Washington drew up his tattered, hungry, and freezing men along the same river bank, roughly opposite Trenton. The conditions may not have been as bad here as at Dunk's ferry, but there couldn't have been too much difference. The men stared at the boats, then at the islands of ice, then at each other. They shook their heads and stamped their chilblained feet.

They also knew why they were there. They were to cross to the other side and attack the British and Hessians in their Trenton quarters. Perhaps the British would not be so full of Christmas dinner or as drunk as dukes, but they would be surprised by a night attack. British gentlemen from the playing fields of Eton didn't attack at night. They went to bed early and slept late. They did their fighting in daylight.

Still, the soldiers thought, there *was* all that ice. They shivered, and stamped, and waited for General Washington to invite them back to camp.

The invitation never came. The General had two things in his favor: a mind that could "even flourish upon care" and an ace up his sleeve. The ace was in the big, heavy, paper parcel he had shown Dr. Rush. He had a boyish-looking aide,

a captain of artillery, bring the parcel to him and break it
open. A cascade of pamphlets spilled out in the slush. The
aide picked up one and squinted at it curiously in the dusk.
His lips moved as he read the title page: *The American
Crisis,* Philadelphia, December 19, 1776. He looked up at
General Washington.

"Captain Hamilton," the General said, "have these pamphlets distributed among the lieutenants and sergeants, one
copy to each, or as far as they will go. Tell them the pamphlet
is to be read to their men." He glanced at the other members of his staff. "You gentlemen will please help Captain
Hamilton in the distribution."

A young lieutenant stepped forward, picked up a copy and
moved away a few yards to a group of soldiers. Sneezing and
coughing, they looked curiously at the pamphlet in the lieutenant's hand. "The General wishes me to read this to you,
men," the lieutenant said. He thumbed back to the last page.
"It is signed by Common Sense."

"That must be old Tom," one of the men said. "What's
he call it?"

"The American Crisis," the lieutenant said, and began to
read:

> "These are the times that try men's souls: The sum-
> mer soldier and the sunshine patriot will, in this
> crisis, shrink from the service of his country; but
> he that stands it NOW, deserves the love and thanks
> of man and woman."

The sneezing and coughing had ceased, the chilblained
feet had stopped shuffling in the slush. A few yards farther
on, the halting voice of a sergeant was soon reading:

> " . . . Tyranny, like hell, is not easily conquered;
> yet we have this consolation with us, that the hard-
> er the conflict, the more glorious the triumph."

And in a minute or so down the line another few yards another sergeant was reading:

> "... What we obtain too cheap, we esteem too lightly; 'Tis dearness only that gives every thing its value. Heaven knows how to set a proper price upon its goods; and it would be strange indeed, if so celestial an article as FREEDOM should not be highly rated."

As each reading was completed, the hush that had fallen on the chilled men continued. There was no applause, but here and there a soldier nodded solemnly to a fellow soldier and clapped him heavily on the back.

Night fell, and the waiting began — hours of it. The waiting after the "hurry-up" that is the life of a soldier, the times that try men's souls ... And at last the waiting ended. When the order came, the men piled into the boats with an eager rush and pulled silently toward Trenton, their faces wet with freezing sleet. Cold and miserable as they were, it warmed their hearts to know that somewhere, in one of the leading boats, was the man they had heard old Tom describe in the dusk of Christmas:

> "... There is a natural firmness in some minds which cannot be unlocked by trifles, but which, when unlocked, discovers a cabinet of fortitude ...

The countersign on this memorable night was "Victory or Death."

The execution of Washington's plan was as brilliant as its conception. The Americans struck during the early hours of December 26. After their Christmas celebration, the British and Hessians alike were in no shape to sustain an attack by the lean, hungry and inspired Americans. A thousand Hessians staggered blearily to their feet, and suffered themselves to be captured. Three British regiments beat a hasty retreat. Washington's winter soldiers set up advance posts, went back to their boats, loaded them with captured equipment and prisoners, rowed back through the islands of ice, and marched into camp, deserving the love and thanks of man and woman.

When it heard of the victory at Trenton, the Congress recovered its morale and took a new lease on life.

CADWALADER's Pennsylvania militia managed to cross the Delaware on December 27. By December 30, they were encamped at Crosswicks. Two days later — on New Year's Day, 1777 — Rush rode to Trenton, to which Washington had returned, and dined with General Hugh Mercer. Mercer filled him in on the details of the First Battle of Trenton.

On the evening of the same day Washington received news of the British intention to attack at both Trenton and Crosswicks. He immediately called a council of war to decide how best to meet the attack. The council was divided. Some favored calling the militia to Trenton. Others wanted to leave it at Crosswicks in order to divide the British force. General Henry Knox — later Secretary of War — suggested that Rush be called in for his opinion. When Rush arrived, Washington summarized the division in the council.

"What do you think we ought to do, Dr. Rush?" he asked.

"I am not a soldier, General," Rush said, "and cannot give a military opinion, but I can assure you that the militia would be happy to be under your immediate command. They would instantly obey a summons to join your troops in Trenton."

Washington thanked him, and Rush withdrew from the council. A few minutes later he was called in again. Washington handed him a letter and asked him to carry it to Cadwalader at Crosswicks.

The major commanding the militia's patrols failed to recognize Rush in the darkness and offered to blow a hole through his chest. He relented when Rush told him his name. Rush rode on. At headquarters he awakened the General and handed him the letter. It ordered Cadwalader and his militia to Trenton. They moved out immediately, on the morning of January 2.

Rush rode on ahead and arrived at Trenton at about seven in the morning. Just as he was falling asleep in General St. Clair's quarters, an alarm gun went off outside the door. Rush jumped up as St. Clair entered, his face calm.

"What's the matter?" Rush asked.

"The enemy are advancing," the General said.

"What are you going to do?"

"Fight 'em," St. Clair said, and buckled on his sword.

Rush followed the General out of the house, mounted his horse, rode to meet the militia, and rode back toward Trenton with them.

"How do you feel?" he asked a militiaman.

"Like I was goin' to sit down to a good breakfast," the man said.

So this was the way generals and soldiers acted on the eve of battle, was it? Cool as cucumbers? Things changed once the Second Battle of Trenton got into full swing. A cannonade began in the afternoon. Men began to fall. Now all was noise and confusion. General Washington and his aides, including Captain Alexander Hamilton, rode by "in all the terrible aspect of war." Looking "all soul" and courage, Rush's old fellow rebel, General Mifflin, galloped by at the head of a body of militia, yelling to the men to get a move on.

Towards evening the battle petered out. The Americans retired from the field, leaving the British once more in possession of Trenton.

Rush had seen his first combat. "It was now," he wrote,

"for the first time war appeared to me in its awful plenitude of horrors." His first battle patient was a New Englander. "His right hand hung a little above his wrist by nothing but a piece of skin. It had been broken by a cannon ball." Rush, together with an older doctor and several young surgeons, "lay down on some straw in the same room with our wounded patients" and listened to their "cries and groans," watched their convulsions.

The battle had been confused. What followed was more so. News came to the doctors that Washington's army had disappeared, no one knew where. Maybe it had gone to Bordentown. It seemed the likeliest guess. The doctors loaded their wounded in wagons, told the drivers to follow, and set off in pursuit. The army was not at Bordentown, but the doctors could hear firing somewhere in the distance. The next morning they discovered what had happened. Washington, on his way to Morristown, had run into part of the British army at Princeton and whipped it. This was on January 3.

The doctors set off in pursuit again. Near Princeton they "passed over the field of battle still red in many places with human blood." On the field they found "a number of wounded officers and soldiers belonging to both armies." One was General Mercer, another Captain McPherson, a British officer. The doctors had the wounded men carried into town. Mercer, who had been badly bayoneted and struck over the head with a musket, died a week later. When Rush went into McPherson's room to examine him, the two men were introduced to each other. McPherson, wounded in the lungs and spitting blood, coughed when he spoke.

"Dr. Rush?" he said. "Benjamin Rush?"

"Yes, Captain."

"The friend of William Leslie, Lord Leven's son?"

"Yes, sir."

"He loved you like a brother."

"And I loved him, sir," Rush said. "You know that he died in the fight yesterday?"

"Yes."

"In his pocket they found a letter from me," Rush said. "He will be buried with the honors of war."

Several years later Rush visited William Leslie's grave. He plucked a blade of grass from it, and erected a headstone inscribed with his name, lineage and record. Then he went home and wrote a letter to Lady Jane, Leslie's sister, telling her he had done so.

WHILE at Princeton Rush saw his father-in-law, Richard Stockton, "who had been plundered of all his household furniture and stock by the British army, and carried a prisoner to New York, from whence he was permitted to return to his family upon parole."

At the end of January, 1777, after his wounded patients were out of danger, Rush felt it was time to attend to his duties in Congress, and set out for Baltimore. On the way he passed a few days with his wife in Maryland.

 16. At War

FROM BALTIMORE, Congressman Rush was pleased to report to Julia that "when the account came to the Congress of your Papa's harsh treatment by General Howe, they immediately ordered General Washington to remonstrate against it and to threaten to inflict similar indignities upon some tory prisoners." This was the only good news he reported from the temporary capital, which was rainy, muddy, crowded and twice as expensive as Philadelphia.

Congress held its last Baltimore session on February 27, 1777. This was also Rush's last session as a congressman. Earlier in the month the Pennsylvania Assembly had failed to re-elect him. His ouster was due to his hostility toward the new Pennsylvania constitution — in particular toward its provision for a one-chamber legislature. "All governments," he maintained, remembering what he had learned from

Montesquieu's *Spirit of Laws*, "are dangerous and tyrannical in proportion as they approach to simplicity." Without a second body to check and balance it, the Pennsylvania Assembly, he thought, had now become tyrannical. Two years later he was to organize the Republican Society to revise the Pennsylvania constitution, but in early 1777 he had other work to do.

On April 11, he was commissioned surgeon general of the Middle Department, which extended from the Hudson to the Potomac. The ten months he spent in the army medical service — up to January 30, 1778, when he resigned — were months of strife and turmoil of soul for Rush. He was simultaneously involved in three different controversies: (1) monetary inflation, (2) Washington's fitness to be commander-in-chief, and (3) the maladministration of the army hospitals. The third controversy, started and led by Rush, is our immediate concern.

THOUGH he was only thirty-one at the time, no American physician was better qualified by aptitude or by training and experience than Rush was to perform the duties of his post. In addition to his natural gifts and excellent training, Rush had had experience on the medical committee of Congress, had served as surgeon of the fleet of Delaware river gunboats, and had treated wounded men after the battles of Trenton and Princeton. Also his powers of observation were unequalled.

The soldiers suffered and died from many scourges, particularly a great variety of fevers — putrid fever, camp fever, hospital fever, jail fever. These were among the several names by which typhus fever was then known, and there was no inoculation for them. They were, therefore, dreaded even more than smallpox. Rush made a number of observations about their spread. Many more cases, he observed, developed when troops of northern, middle and southern states were together in one encampment. He noted that fever seemed to be carried by blankets and clothing when men returned to camp from a hospital. There was more illness under crowded tent conditions than in the open, and more among troops quartered in private houses than among barrack troops. Men under thirty succumbed more readily than men over thirty; more native Americans than Europeans; more Negroes than whites; more men with rheumatism or pleurisy than men free of these diseases. Well-clad officers were more resistant than ragged soldiers.

These scientific observations were made over many months and in many places. Immediate concrete evidence of Rush's qualifications was the publication in the *Pennsylvania Packet* of his "Directions for Preserving the Health of Soldiers." This appeared just eleven days after he received his first commission. The "Directions" asserted "that the mortality from sickness in camps is not necessarily connected with a soldier's life." The truth of the assertion has now long been recognized, but in 1777 Rush was proclaiming a novel doctrine. The "Directions" was pioneer work in American military hygiene, still another of Rush's many "firsts." It was republished in pamphlet form in 1778, reissued at least twice during the Civil War, and reprinted as late as 1908. It was a classic for well over a century.

While with the Pennsylvania militia and with Washington's troops at Trenton and Princeton, Rush had seen with his own eyes the shocking filth and neglect, in which men lived in army camps. In the "Directions" he urged that every soldier wash his hands and face at least once a day, comb his hair, bathe two or three times a week, change clothes often, air and sun his blankets, and not sleep in wet clothes. Kitchens and kitchen utensils, he said, must be kept clean, areas around tents and encampments kept free from garbage and other refuse. Camp sites should be changed frequently and located at some distance from marshes and ponds. The diet should include well-cooked vegetables. Rum should be rarely used and then only as medicine. Physical exercise should be a regular part of army routine.

Today these measures are standard operating procedure, but during the Revolution, and for a long time afterward in America, soldiers, officers and even many doctors considered them hare-brained and fanciful. The "Directions" and his observations on the health of men at war contributed much to Rush's later recognition as early America's most eminent physician — America's first really great physician; the first name entered in the Medical Hall of Fame, now graced with such names as Walter B. Cannon and Harvey Cushing.

THE medical department of the Continental Army labored under a disheartening assortment of handicaps. America was an infant country, inexperienced in large-scale war, and backward in medicine, even by the low standards then prevailing in England and Continental Europe. To make things worse, instruments, supplies, funds and hospital beds were pitifully scarce. New York was held by the British, so that the permanent hospital there was unavailable. The Pennsylvania Hospital, the only other permanent one, was also unavailable while Philadelphia was in British hands.

Rush and the other doctors had to make do with makeshift and hopelessly inadequate facilities. Almost always the "hospital" was a hastily and crazily built log hut or shack with a dirt floor and a fireplace in the center. The smoke escaped, if it did, through a hole in the roof. Or the hospital was an inn, a farmhouse, a church or school building. A few lucky or high-ranking patients perhaps lay in beds. The rest — in ragged, filthy clothes and without proper or sufficient food or medicines — lay cheek by jowl on the bare floor or on filthy, infested straw pallets. If a man didn't have a disease when he entered the hospital, his floormates soon provided him with one.

Another handicap was that from the very beginning of the war, the army medical department was badly organized. The hospital plan for an army of 20,000 men called for: a director general and chief physician, four surgeons, twenty surgeon's assistants, one apothecary, two men in charge of materials, and one nurse for every ten patients. Later the number of surgeons and assistants was increased, but never enough.

As Rush and others saw it, the duties of the director general were too heavy for one man to bear. The director general, with the exception of the first one, was both chief physician and purveyor general of supplies and medicines — functions that the experienced armies of England and Europe had found incompatible and conducive to waste and corruption.

This was bad enough, but the problem was compounded by a long-drawnout feud. In July, 1775, Dr. Benjamin Church became the first director general. Three months later he was court-martialed for treasonous activity and dismissed. Dr. John Morgan succeeded him immediately. This was the honest, capable and fearless John Morgan whose medical bag, Dr. Redman had once told his apprentice Benjamin Rush, he might one day be worthy of carrying. It was *the* John Morgan who drove Dr. William Shippen, Jr., berserk when Morgan established the Medical College of Philadelphia in 1765, and who brought back an apothecary from England to the detriment of the pill-rolling profits of Philadelphia physicians, including William Shippen, Jr.

Perhaps Congress and the army brass were not aware of the old Morgan-Shippen feud. At any rate they poured oil on its still-glowing embers when they made Shippen co-director with Morgan in October, 1776. Morgan's sphere was to be east of the Hudson, Shippen's west. Shippen — who had considerable influence in Congress, what with his marriage into the powerful Lee family of Virginia — lost no time in undermining his old enemy. It took him only three months. Morgan was dismissed as director general in January, 1777. Congress gave no reason for the action. From then on Shippen was sole director general — also chief physician and purveyor general.

Shippen, then, was boss when Rush was commissioned surgeon general in April. It was the William Shippen, Jr., who had kept students away from Rush's chemistry lectures and who, Jacob Rush had once said was a man "of cool malice and treachery" with whom, Jacob had advised, it was well "to be at eternal variance."

Jacob's now-ancient advice was hardly necessary. Being at variance with William Shippen, Jr., came naturally to Rush. And if you put an unscrupulous person like Shippen at the head of a bad medical organization you had a chaotic combination. Rush flew at both with his customary verve and tenacity of purpose.

But not immediately. It is difficult to understand, but at first Rush seems not to have grasped the problem of the bad hospital conditions. On August 8, 1777 — four months after he entered the service, a month after being promoted to physician general — he wrote to Congressman John Adams from Morristown: "I have the pleasure of informing you that great order, cleanliness, and the most perfect contentment prevail in our hospitals."

His eyes popped open in Bethlehem, Pennsylvania. The huge Brethren House of the Moravian Church there had become a hospital and a happy hunting ground for disease-carrying vermin, including the typhus louse. The more than seven hundred men crowded into this charnel house would have been safer in a hail of bullets. During the last three months of 1777 more than a third of the men died. On his first visit, Rush was conducted through the putrid rooms by Dr. William Smith. The sick men lay on filthy straw pallets within inches of each other. Smith and Rush stopped beside the pallet of a man who had recently died. As they were looking down at the man, Smith stooped over, peered at something, then raised his foot and brought it down smartly on the floor.

He straightened up. "Typhus louse," he explained. "It was moving on to the next man. When a body becomes cold and unpleasant, these typhus fellows shift to a living man."

"How often are you able to change pallets?" Rush asked.

"Oh, we're generally able to get a new pallet after four or five men have died on one," Dr. Smith said.

"They're infected with lice, then, almost all the time?"

"That's right."

"Of course you have complained to Dr. Shippen," Rush said.

"To the director general?" Smith laughed bitterly. "He assures us everything is shipshape, Doctor."

A hospital orderly entered the room, his face haggard from fatigue, his eyes bloodshot from lack of sleep. In each hand he carried a pewter mug. Rush stopped him and placed a hand on his brow.

"You have a fever," Rush said. "You ought to be in bed."

The orderly's laugh was bitter, too. "Yes, sir," he said.

"What's that you have in the mugs?" Rush asked.

"Madeira, sir, for two of the patients."

"Here, let me see." Rush dipped the corner of a clean linen handkerchief in one of the mugs, put it in his mouth and sucked it. He turned to Dr. Smith. "This wine is adulterated — badly adulterated."

Smith laughed again as the orderly walked away. "Adulterated, you say, Doctor? You should taste some of the stuff we get from the purveyor general. Our present stock is high proof by comparison."

"But this is no medicine for men as sick as these." Rush said.

"You should speak to Dr. Shippen, sir. This is what he sends us."

"I intend to," Rush said. "Is he still here in Bethlehem?"

"I am told he has been here for the past six weeks, but he has not honored us with a visit."

"Hasn't set foot in this hospital for six weeks!" Rush started for the door.

"You won't complain of *his* madeira, Dr. Rush. His is full strength and plentiful — unless that wagon train that left here yesterday was carrying his last load."

"Wagon train! Do you mean to tell me he ships whole wagon-train loads of it for his own use, while these poor fellows are dying for the want of it?"

"Oh, it's all shipshape, sir. These are government wagons."

"Government wagons! Why, this — why, this is — " The missing word may have been "treason."

An emaciated, bleary-eyed soldier staggered into the room, tottered to an empty pallet and flopped down on it. He closed his eyes and began to snore.

Rush stared down at him. "That man is drunk!" he said.

"Drunk as a duke, Doctor. Perhaps he tired of our pap." He nodded toward two other happy snorers. "Two more dukes," he said.

"But where are your officers and guards?"

"With the army. The chief physician, who is a general officer, says we don't need any, and the other general officers seem to agree."

Rush started for the door again, then turned back to Dr. Smith. "We must have discipline!" he said.

Smith pretended a look of shock. "Discipline, Doctor?" he said. "Would you have us give up our American freedom?"

THIS type of experience enabled Rush to make an important discovery, which he revealed in a letter to General Nathanael Greene from the hospital at Lancaster, near Bethlehem, Pennsylvania. "I have made a discovery," he wrote, " — a sure and certain method of destroying Howe's whole army without powder or ball or without any of the common implements of death. Lead them through any of the villages in Lancaster county where we have a hospital, and I will ensure you that in six weeks there shall not be a man of them alive or fit for duty."

His eyes were further opened after Washington's defeat at Brandywine on September 11, 1777. During the battle Rush was nearly captured, when he remained too long on the battlefield to take care of the wounded. After the battle Washington sent Rush and several surgeons with a flag of truce into General Howe's camp to attend wounded American captives. The experience gave him a chance to compare British with American field hospitals.

The "perfect contentment" he had earlier reported in American hospitals, he now found in British hospitals. Even wounded Americans, though thoroughly hated, he wrote to John Adams, were treated better by General Howe's medical department after Brandywine than by their own. The British "care of our wounded," he said, "was entirely the effect of their medical establishment, which mechanically forced happiness and satisfaction upon our countrymen." Because of the discipline enforced by officers and guards, the patients in the British hospital did no rambling or drinking and, therefore, did not contract new diseases nor prolong the ones they had. In the hospital at Trenton, where his letter was written two weeks after Brandywine, he reported, "upwards of 100 [patients] were drunk last night. We have no guards to prevent this evil." The debauchery, he claimed, was "all the effects of *our* medical establishment," which, besides, was full of waste and thievery in high places. "It is now universally said," he went on, "that the system was formed for the Director General and not for the benefit of the sick and wounded."

This letter, written on October 1, 1777, five days after the British occupation of Philadelphia, was the opening gun in Rush's campaign against the medical department. The sentence about the director general may be interpreted merely as criticism of the too-great powers granted to anyone who might hold the office, that is, as criticism of "the system" only. But, considering what Rush knew by that time of the director general's sticky fingers and neglect of duty, the implied criticism of Dr. William Shippen was thinly veiled.

In another letter to Adams, written at Reading three weeks later, he left no doubt about his meaning: "Our hospital affairs grow worse and worse," he wrote. "The fault is both in the establishment and in the Director General. He is both *ignorant* and *negligent* of his duty." He went on to ask whether there was any hope of a Congressional reorganization of the department. "Dr. [William] Brown and every medical officer in the hospital execrate it," he said. "If it cannot be altered, and that soon, I shall trouble you with my resignation, and my reasons shall afterwards be given to the public for it." Adams was evidently too busy to help. Washington was also busy — keeping an army alive at Valley Forge.

At the time of this letter to Adams, Rush was just warming to his work. By December 13, when he wrote to William Duer, a congressman from New York, he was red hot. "I wish some members of Congress (not related to Dr. S-----n) would visit our hospitals and converse with the principal surgeons in them. Dr. S---n has taken great pains to extort the power of appointment out of the physician and surgeon general's hands, and has made some of them dependent on his will, yet I believe you will not find more than *one* man among them who does not reprobate our system and who will not ring peals of distress and villainy in your ears much louder than anything you have heard from me." This was no exaggeration. Two months later, four doctors at the Brethren House in Bethlehem signed a blistering affidavit testifying to the heinousness of Shippen's neglectful and plundering ways.

Rush did more than call attention to abuses. He also proposed remedies. He proposed that an inspector general and chief physician should be appointed to examine all hospitals, to check on the quantity and quality of medicines, instruments and other supplies, and to keep an account of the number of sick and wounded. A purveyor general, having nothing to do with the actual care of the sick, would provide the hospitals with supplies. Only the physicians and surgeons general, who were close to the sick and knew what they needed, were to administer the stores provided by the purveyor, who would honor only written orders. All expense vouchers were to be countersigned by the physicians.

It was inevitable that Rush's criticism should reach Shippen's ears. And it was inevitable that Shippen should charge Rush with wanting Shippen's job. In another letter to Duer, Rush denied the charge, once more clearly implied that Shippen was a villain, and again threatened to resign.

The two letters to Duer, together with a letter from Governor William Livingston of New Jersey on the hospital uproar, were referred to a committee headed by none other than Rush's old friend John Witherspoon, president of the College of New Jersey. The committee recommended that Rush and Shippen attend Congress on January 26, 1778, "to be examined." While awaiting the examination, the two continued to snarl at each other. Shippen accused Rush of ignorance and neglect of duty and was also — Rush wrote Julia — busy lobbying in Congress. As a counter-punch Rush, after fruitlessly appealing to Shippen himself, went over Shippen's head and wrote to Washington. The letter once more raked the medical department over the coals but did not explicitly attack Shippen. In his letter to Julia, however, written three weeks later, Rush said that he had prepared his charge against Shippen and that if Congress supported the director general, he would resign "in a few weeks."

On January 25, Rush wrote to Henry Laurens, president of the Congress, asking that the examination of himself and Shippen be a *"public* hearing" before the whole Congress instead of before Witherspoon's committee. The letter was read to the Congress the next day, and on the day after that all pertinent letters, including Rush's and Shippen's, were referred back to the committee, which denied the request for a public hearing. It then examined the two doctors as originally planned. Afterward Witherspoon told Rush that the committee could not endorse the sweeping reforms Rush had proposed. It was the committee's belief that the feud could be resolved only by the resignation of either Rush or Shippen.

Presumably Shippen had no intention of resigning, so Rush resigned — on January 30, 1778. Witherspoon wrote Rush that his resignation "was accepted without a word said by any Person upon the Subject." A day or so later Richard Peters, secretary of the Board of War, wrote Robert Morris that the hospital department was "convulsed to its Center. Rush has resigned."

AT the time of Peters' letter, it was doubtless impossible for anyone outside the medical department to know just where the truth lay. Present knowledge, however, makes it reason-

able to believe that it lay overwhelmingly on Rush's side.
It seems clear, for example, that Shippen did misappropriate
and often sold hospital wine and other supplies, that he did
consistently avoid hospitals, and that he did submit rosy reports on the number of sick and dead.

In the same ironic letter to General Greene in which he
said he had discovered a way of "destroying Howe's whole
army without powder or ball," Rush's irony destroyed the
validity of Shippen's death reports:

> "I find from examining Dr. Shippen's return of the
> numbers who die in the hospitals that I was mis-
> taken in the accounts I gave of that matter in my
> letters to you. From his return of December last I
> find very few have died in proportion to the number
> I have mentioned. All I can say in apology for this
> mistake is that I was deceived by counting the num-
> ber of coffins that were daily put under ground.
> From their weight and smell I am persuaded they
> contained hospital patients in them, and if they were
> not dead I hope some steps will be taken for the
> future to prevent and punish the crime of burying
> the Continental soldiers alive. It is a new evil under
> the sun, and I hope a new punishment will be dis-
> covered for it."

Rush seems to have had Shippen and the medical department dead to rights on all major counts of his indictment.

AFTER his resignation Rush went to Morven in Princeton,
where Julia and their son, John, were living. The quiet rus-
ticity of the place was no medicine for a fire-ship like Rush.
Philadelphia was still in the hands of the British, and Rush
couldn't abide the idea of becoming a country doctor. "In

this situation," he wrote in his *Autobiography,* "I resolved
to study the law, and come forward to the bar in New Jersey." Richard Stockton, his father-in-law, encouraged the
idea. But then, in May, 1778, the British evacuated Philadelphia, and in June Rush, Julia and John returned to the
city. "The filth left by the British Army in the streets," he
wrote, "created a good deal of sickness. I quickly recovered
my business, with a large accession of new patients." He became ill from overwork and worry, but slowly recovered. "I
now turned my back for a while upon public pursuits," he
said, "and devoted myself exclusively to the duties of my
profession."

BUT he could not turn his back on the Shippen affair. It
dragged on for another three years. In April, 1778, Congress
had appointed a second committee of inquiry, which was to
submit a report. Rush now took the position that Shippen's
misconduct was not a Congressional matter. Shippen, he
pointed out in a letter to the committee, was an army officer
and should be tried by court-martial. Early in June the letter
was read to the Congress and tabled.

A few days later Congress finally got around to exonerating
Dr. John Morgan. Congress instructed Washington to have
Morgan's charges investigated. While the investigation
limped along, Morgan gathered evidence and repeatedly
urged Congress to take action. At Morgan's request Rush
enumerated the charges on which he was willing to testify in
court.

At long last — on March 14, 1780 — Shippen's court-
martial got under way at Morristown. Including a month's re-
cess at its half-way point, the trial lasted two and a half
months. On the stand Rush testified against William Shippen, Jr., for three days running. The formal charges were
that Shippen had sold hospital stores as his own property,

speculated in hospital stores "whilst the sick were perishing for want of them," failed to keep proper accounts, neglected his hospital duties, and engaged in other "Scandalous and infamous practices such as are unbecoming the Character of an Officer & Gentleman."

It is a wry commentary on the way of the world and of men in high places with the right connections that the court formally acquitted Shippen, though several years later one of the court told Rush that "there was a majority of but a single vote in favor of his acquittal." An added touch of wryness — even of cynicism — is that the acquittal was granted despite the court's upholding of the second charge "that doctor Shippen did speculate in and sell hospital stores, THAT is, stores proper for hospitals, whilst he was purveyor general: which conduct they consider highly improper, and justly reprehensible." Nevertheless, Shippen went free.

Washington transmitted the trial record to Congress on July 15, 1780, without any personal comments. After long debate, Congress refused to approve the acquittal but ordered that Shippen "be discharged from arrest." Shortly afterwards Congress reinstated Shippen as director general. Then, as a kind of confession that Rush had been right in his criticism, Congress ordered into effect some of his most important reform suggestions: separation of the administrative and supply functions of the director general; more authority to the physicians and officers in charge of the hospitals; a more accurate accounting of finances and figures on the number of sick and dead.

Shippen's discharge from arrest officially closed the case. It did not close the debate between Shippen on the one side and Rush and Morgan on the other. It went on bitterly for another four months in the columns of the *Pennsylvania Packet*.

The reason for Washington's noncommittal attitude toward the trial can only be guessed at. During the trial he had had Rush to dinner at his headquarters, and all accounts indicate that the atmosphere was congenial. When he transmitted the trial record to Congress, then, how could so just a man fail to reveal his feelings toward so flagrant a miscarriage of justice? The answer may be that back in 1777 Rush had been somewhat indiscreet in his criticism of Washington's conduct of the war and this resulted in what a modern historian has called the "unfortunate and unseemly" quarrel between Rush and Washington.

17. "Unseemly" Quarrel with the Commander-in-Chief

"THERE IS NOTHING MYSTERIOUS ABOUT" the quarrel, the editor of the *Letters of Benjamin Rush* writes. "If one can rid one's mind of certain traditions of Revolutionary history, long standard but not well supported by evidence, the basic cause of the quarrel stands out clearly: Rush was given to reckless criticism, and Washington was extremely sensitive to any kind of criticism. Both men had justification for their mutual resentment, though neither fully understood the causes of the other's feeling. The incident reflects little credit on Washington and still less on Rush, who was, however, to pay a far greater penalty than his indiscretion merited."

How did the misunderstanding between Rush and Washington come about and how much justification was there for it on both sides?

ODDLY enough the good relations between Rush and Wash-

ington during the first three years of their acquaintance
were later transformed by Washington into a reason for
breaking with Rush in 1778. Rush admired Washington
when the two first met in 1774. His admiration also sounds
in his account of the dinner in June, 1775, celebrating Washington's appointment as commander-in-chief. Later in the
same year Rush paid a handsome tribute to Washington in
an unsigned letter to his old schoolmate, Dr. Thomas Ruston:
"You would distinguish him," he wrote, "to be a general and
a soldier from among ten thousand people. There is not a
king in Europe that would not look like a valet de chambre
by his side."

Ruston was in London at the time, which explains why the
letter was unsigned. Rush merely wished to keep his identity
a secret from the British in case they intercepted the letter,
which they did. As a matter of fact, Rush had a habit — like
nearly all correspondents at the time — of not signing letters
even when circumstances did not call for not signing. The
practice is stressed here only because another and more famous of Rush's unsigned letters was the chief cause of his
break with Washington.

There is further evidence of Rush's early high opinion of
Washington. During the fighting around Trenton, in 1776,
Rush was so struck by Washington's abilities and character
that on December 30 he suggested to Richard Henry Lee
that Washington should be given dictatorial powers — "or,"
he wrote, "we are undone." The good relations continued
well into 1777, when the two men exchanged letters on
smallpox inoculation and other army health matters.

Similar praise for Washington was given by many others,
with no reason to suppose it was anything but genuine. Rush's
praise was equally genuine. But after the first flood of adula-
tion, the tide began to ebb. One reason was that civil leaders
were afraid the military would come to dominate over civil
power. Rush shared this fear. In April, 1777, an entry in his

notebook deplores the fact that Washington "is idolized by the people of America and is thought to be absolutely necessary to enable us to carry on the war." Discontent with this idolatry for the General grew and spread throughout Washington's military and political career.

In the same entry in his notebook already quoted, Rush wrote: "I think it more than probable that General Washington will not close the present war with G. Britain." One reason was that Washington's "talents are unequal to those degrees of discipline and decision which alone can render an army finally successful."

Then, after Rush had observed the conditions in such hospitals as the one at Bethlehem and had had a chance after Brandywine to compare them with what he considered the exemplary management of the British hospitals, he observed a similar absence of discipline in the army. On October 1, 1777, three days before Germantown, he wrote to John Adams from Trenton: "In my way to this place I passed through General Washington's army. To my great mortification I arrived at the headquarters of a general on an outpost without being challenged by a single sentry. I saw soldiers straggling from our lines in every quarter without an officer, exposed every moment to be picked up by the enemy's light horse. I heard of 2,000 who sneaked off . . . to Bethlehem. I was told by a captain in our army that they would not be missed . . . and that . . . General Washington never knew within 3,000 men what his real numbers were. I saw nothing but confidence about headquarters and languor in all branches and extremities of the army."

Nine days after the defeat at Germantown, Rush wrote once more to Adams: "We lost a city, a victory, a campaign by that want of discipline and system which pervades every part of the army." He went on to say that General Thomas Conway, after whom the supposed conspiracy against Wash-

ington was named, and who was threatening to resign because he had not been promoted to major general, "wept for
joy when he saw the ardor with which our troops pushed the
enemy from hill to hill, and pronounced our country free
from that auspicious sight. But when he saw an officer low in
command give counterorders to the Commander-in-Chief,
and the Commander-in-Chief passive under the circumstance,
his distress and resentment exceeded all bounds. For God's
sake, do not suffer him to resign." Conway, Rush concluded,
"is exact in his discipline and understands every part of the
detail of an army." As a matter of fact, Conway — an Irish-
man who had achieved the rank of colonel in the experienced
French army — evidently was a competent officer and a first-
rate trainer of troops.

Rush was only one of many civil leaders at this time who
took a dim view of Washington's ability as a disciplinarian.
They also believed he had made serious mistakes in the field,
and were convinced that many besides his close "military
family" were touchy about any criticism of him. It was unwise, John Adams thought, to look upon Washington as "a
deity or a savior." Congressman Thomas Burke of North
Carolina thought the Germantown defeat had "sprung from
the usual source — want of abilities in our superior officers
and want of order and discipline in our army."

By no means did all of the criticism come from civilians.
Colonel Daniel Brodhead of Pennsylvania, about a month
after Germantown, wrote to General Horatio Gates, victor at
the Battle of Saratoga early in October: "Since you left us our
Division has suffered greatly and that chiefly by the conduct
of Gen'l W———n. Most of the officers are unhappy under his
command."

Rush had the misfortune of backing all the wrong people
so far as Washington and his supporters were concerned. On
October 21, 1777, he wrote John Adams: "I have heard sev-

eral officers who have served under General Gates compare his
army to a well-regulated family. The same g⌐ntlemen have
compared General Washington's imitation of an army to an
unformed mob." He went on to contrast Gates's successes in
northern New York with Washington's failures in Pennsylvania.

HOWEVER misguided Rush may have been in his estimate of
military affairs, the patriotic foundation of his zeal is no
longer in question. In military matters he was simply out of
his depth. But he was thoroughly qualified to judge medical
affairs. He could easily concur in the criticism of Washington
as a disciplinarian because he had observed the lack of discipline in the hospitals with a highly trained professional eye.
In not cracking down on William Shippen, Jr., and the medical department, Washington — Rush may have felt — was
characteristically shirking his responsibility for discipline
throughout his command.

When Rush failed to get remedial action on the hospitals
by writing to John Adams, Shippen, and Congressman Duer,
he wrote to Washington himself for help. This letter of
December 26, 1777, has been called "a model statement and
plea of its kind." In his letter Rush complained, legitimately,
that Shippen refused to delegate authority to doctors actually
in the hospitals. Governor Livingston of New Jersey wrote
a similar letter at about the same time. Washington answered
Livingston on December 31, but delayed answering Rush
until January 12.

By an ironic historical accident Washington replied to
Rush on the same day that Rush once again proved that he
considered prudence "a *rascally virtue*." For on this same
January 12, 1778, Rush wrote to Governor Patrick Henry of
Virginia, and thereby got his name connected with what has
come to be known as the "Conway Cabal." This was another

of Rush's unsigned letters. "The author of it," Rush told
Henry, "is one of your Philadelphia friends ... The letter
must be thrown in the fire. But some of its contents ought
to be made public in order to awaken, enlighten, and alarm
our country."

In not signing the letter, Rush was not attempting to keep
his identity a secret from Patrick Henry. He was fairly sure
that Henry would recognize the characteristic Rush sentiments if not the handwriting.

At any rate the letter was dynamite. America's "army —
what is it?" Rush asked. "A major general [that is, John
Sullivan] belonging to it called it a few days ago in my hearing a *mob*. Discipline unknown, or *wholly* neglected." Rush
goes on to enumerate the many things that were deteriorat-
ing outside, as well as inside the army. "But is our case desperate?" he asked. "By no means. We have wisdom, virtue,
and strength *enough* to save us if they could be called into
action."

Whatever Patrick Henry may have thought about Washington's talents early in the war, and whatever he thought
of them when he received Rush's letter, he evidently believed the commander-in-chief deserved to see the letter.
Henry, therefore, forwarded it to him.

Some weeks later Washington wrote to Henry. "The Anonymous Letter with which you were pleased to favour me,"
he said, "was written by Doctor Rush, so far as I can judge
from a similitude of hands. This Man has been elaborate,
and studied in his professions of regard for me; and long
since the Letter to you." There then follows the paragraph
on which believers in Washington's infallibility, past and present, have chiefly based their belief in the existence of a "Conway Cabal."

"My caution [Washington wrote] to avoid any thing,

that could injure the service, prevented me from communicating, but to very few of my friends, the intrigues of a faction, which I know was formed against me, since it might serve to publish our internal dissensions; but their own restless zeal to advance their views has too clearly betrayed them, and made concealment, on my part, fruitless. I cannot precisely mark the extent of their views, but it appeared in general, that General Gates was to be exalted, on the ruin of my reputation and influence. This I am authorized to say, from undeniable facts in my own possession, from publications, the evident scope of which, could not be mistaken, and from private detractions industriously circulated. General Mifflin, it is commonly supposed, bore the second part in the Cabal; and General Conway, I know was a very Active and malignant Partisan."

Washington's remark that Rush had "been elaborate, and studied in his professions of regard for me" clearly shows that Washington considered Rush's long-continued deference a cloak to conceal his conspiratorial dagger. For the remark was made in the same letter in which he named what he believed to be the principal military figures in "the Cabal."

At the time Washington wrote to Patrick Henry he was depressed and nervous because of his defeats of the preceding fall and the resultant criticism. He was also much concerned about the condition of his army at Valley Forge, and somewhat doubtful about being able to get it into fighting trim. It is, therefore, understandable that he should believe in the existence of a conspiracy against him.

Rush, to be sure, was one of a large number of critics of Washington. Criticize, however, was all that Rush and the others did. Nor were the civilian critics all New Englanders.

The bitterest criticism from civilians came from Pennsylvania and New Jersey leaders, who felt that Washington had not given them sufficient protection. Many in Pennsylvania contended that a "people's army," a militia, could do a better job than Washington's "professional" army.

Rush agreed. Like others, he noted that militia had played a major role in the early days of the war and around Saratoga, where Gates had achieved his decisive victory, which was instrumental in persuading France to come to America's assistance. In fact, Rush believed that militia would end the war as militia had begun it.

Rush also wanted a sweeping reformation of the army. He wished to see general officers, who had proved incompetent and who had given Washington bad advice, replaced by others. Many, whose loyalty to Washington has never been questioned, favored Rush's reform proposals — for example, Henry Laurens, president of Congress, General Anthony Wayne, and General Johann Kalb.

In other words, the so-called Conway Cabal appears not to have been the conspiracy Washington thought it was. But though the substance of it was the creation of a much-harried mind, the shadow seemed real enough. There was widespread complaint inside and outside the military. Some was ill-founded, some not. All sorts of knowledgeable, thoughtful complainers really believed, as Rush did, that America was in a bad way. They honestly and patriotically wondered — out loud or in letters — if another man might not be a more reliable savior than Washington. And in the crisis it must have been much easier for Washington to believe that his critics were conspirators than to embrace them like brothers.

LATER relations between Rush and Washington prove that neither man held a lasting resentment, which would indi-

cate that Washington finally concluded that Rush had had
no part in the Cabal, even if Washington continued to believe that a Cabal existed. During Shippen's court-martial in
1780, for example, Washington invited Rush to dine with
him at his Morristown headquarters. Subsequently, there
was an occasional exchange of friendly letters between them.
During the Federal Convention, in 1787, Washington dined
at Rush's home. And when Washington was proposed as first
President, Rush said that Washington was the right man "to
drive our new wagon."

Rush suffered no further change of mind about the first
President himself, but he did agree with men like John Adams
and Thomas Jefferson that Washington was surrounded by
ambitious and unscrupulous advisers. Certainly long before
Washington's retirement, all the old animosity between
Rush and Washington had been long since dead.

18. Raising a Generation
of Doctors

IN MAY, 1778, THE BRITISH finally evacuated Philadelphia, and on June 21 Rush returned to his beloved city. After the trials he had undergone in the Congress, in the militia and in his tussle with William Shippen, Jr., Rush needed rest desperately, but there was no time for that. The British had left Philadelphia a filthy mess, and there was sickness everywhere. Rush plunged into the work of healing with his habitual energy. "I quickly recovered my business," he wrote in his *Autobiography*. He did more than that. His varied efforts in public life and in medicine had made him widely known and respected. The name of Dr. Benjamin Rush had become one to conjure with. New patients flocked to him. Tired as he was, he worked as he had never worked before.

He worked and worried himself to the verge of nervous and physical collapse. Not even Julia and the baby, who came to him from Morven early in August, could buoy him up. In September he caught a "malignant bilious fever" from a patient, and for many days hovered near death. Two of his physicians — Redman, his old preceptor, and Morgan — called on him and thought that he was dying. To cheer his friend's last moments, Morgan assured him that sooner or later he would lift the scalp of William Shippen, Jr., but Rush was too ill to care. The two physicians left the sickroom, with heads bowed and drying their eyes.

"We are losing a good friend, a good man and a good doctor," Redman said.

Morgan nodded. "If he should live — and I'm afraid he can't — one day we will all be glad to become his apprentices. How old is he now?" he asked.

Redman shut his eyes in thought. "Let me see. He was fifteen when he came to me in '61. That would make him thirty-two now. So young to have done so much!" He shook his head. "And I doubted that he would ever become a doctor." He shook his head again. "But what a shame he has abandoned the doctrines of Dr. Boerhaave. Thank heaven he adores that other god of my idolatry, Dr. Sydenham."

"And he resembles Sydenham," Morgan said. "Sydenham was a great observer, a great investigator, a great clinician, and so is Rush."

"No one half so good," Redman agreed. "He will be sorely missed."

"He will — and by none more than by the poor."

Redman brightened a little. "Yes, in his devotion to them he resembles Boerhaave."

"Also in his bloodletting," Morgan said with a faint smile.

The two doctors' sorrow was premature. After making his will and taking leave of life, Rush recovered. By November he was going full blast again, and for Rush, going full blast meant politics as well as medicine. He resumed his old battle against the Pennsylvania constitution by organizing the Republican Society, devoted to its amendment. This brought him into the line of political fire once more, "the subject of much newspaper abuse." But he was happy, for in the midst of a battle, he was in his element.

HE was in two battles. The second one was medical and, in its various phases, it continued to the end of his life, in 1813. The first phase, which began in 1769, when he returned from Edinburgh and London, flaunting the banner of Dr. Cullen in the angry faces of the Boerhaave men, was well over by 1790. By then, most Philadelphia doctors had succumbed to the Cullen system. But by then, Rush had abandoned the Cullen system and substituted his own — the Rush system, based on the ideas of Edinburgh's Dr. John Brown and on his own studies and unmatched clinical observation.

During his Cullen period, which covered nearly two decades, Rush based his theory and practice on Cullen's *Genera Morborum,* "The Kinds of Diseases." According to Cullen, each kind was caused by too much nervous energy (or excitability) or too little. Fever, for example, was caused by too much. But though Cullen recognized only two *causes* of disease, he believed he had identified 1,387 *kinds* of disease. Each kind required a different medicine.

Rush came to disagree. Like William of Occam, back in the fourteenth century, Rush believed that one should "never multiply distinctions beyond necessity," a doctrine that is one of the cornerstones of modern science. Cullen's distinctions among fevers, Rush thought, were multiplied far beyond necessity. Rush said that a fever is a fever. To the careless observer one fever may seem different from other fevers. Snow, ice, frost and dew are also different in appearance, though they are only different forms of the same substance — water. Using an analogous argument, Rush claimed that every fever is only a variant form of the same thing — namely, fever.

In one sense, then, Rush's system was simpler than Cullen's, if no truer. Rush recognized only two kinds of disease. One kind weakened the pulse, the other excited it. In another sense his system was more complicated than Cullen's. For Cullen there were only two causes of disease — too much nervous energy and too little. For Rush there were many causes. To this extent he was nearer the truth than Cullen. He cannot be blamed for not knowing such true causes as germs and viruses, which had not yet been discovered.

Rush's method of cure was just as simple as his two-fold classificetion of disease. A weakened pulse and attendant signs required stimulation in the form of a heavy diet of meat, wine, "spirits" and stimulating drugs. An excited pulse and attendant signs required a moderate diet, sweating, purging — and bloodletting.

Cullen had preached against bloodletting, as his followers continued to do. Their main reliance was on vomits, purges, blisters (raised by plasters), sweats and salivation (the abnormal production of saliva through the use of mercury, as in calomel). Of course, Rush also used these remedies, though he frowned on salivation. Like others, for example, he was devoted to purgatives, and he liked to prescribe jalap, or "elephant's cathartic."

Bloodletting, however, was his preferred remedy. Its virtues were that it reduced a fast pulse and speeded up a slow one, lessened pains in the head, increased sweating, made the body respond to mercury and the bowels to cathartics, cooled a feverish skin, induced sleep, and prevented many chronic diseases. And bloodletting, Rush claimed, was safer than other remedies. "Bleeding should be repeated while the symptoms which first indicated it continue . . . " The number of his followers among younger doctors increased, especially among his former students.

In the course of his career as a teacher, Rush trained more than 3,000 doctors. This number was reinforced by recruits who had received their training elsewhere, or who were simply urged by their patients to seek and follow the advice of Rush, after he had been elevated to the rank of "dean of American medicine."

Even before he had achieved that rank, he was besieged by boys, such as he himself had been in 1761, who wished to become his "apprentices." To save himself for his other work, he limited their number to six, and charged the high fee of £100.

Most of his teaching was done in the lecture hall. After the British evacuation of Philadelphia and the reopening of the College of Philadelphia, he resumed his chemistry lectures. These were interrupted, in 1779, by the suspension of the institution's charter, but were again resumed, in 1781, in the new University of the State of Pennsylvania, where he also lectured on the practice of physic. Through the influence of Franklin and others, the old College of Philadelphia again reopened in 1789, Rush and some former members of the old college staff accepted posts in its medical school. On Morgan's death in 1789. the trustees elected Rush to succeed him in the chair of the theory and practice of medicine. Rush then relinquished his professorship in chemistry. In 1791, the old College of Philadelphia and the University of the State of Pennsylvania merged into the University of Pennsylvania, where Rush became professor of the institutes of medicine and clinical medicine. In 1796, he assumed the additional professorship of the practice of physic. His lectures on the institutes and practice of medicine and his supervision of the medical clinics continued until his death, in 1813.

THE number of Rush-trained doctors was in itself an enormous contribution to American medicine. Though Rush and others still trained apprentices, beginning in the 1770's, the apprentices did not have to complete their education abroad. University training became available in their own country, mainly under three men — Morgan, Shippen and Rush. Before many years had passed, Rush became the most respected of these and the most widely known. His preeminence was deserved. He gave the study and practice of medicine a new dignity — a standing it had conspicuously lacked before his time.

Every student worth his salt recognizes a great teacher, as Rush's students recognized him. Rush did not lecture off the top of his head or from old, stale lecture notes. He kept revising his notes, freshening them up, bringing them up to the minute. He put everything he had into his lectures, and he had more than anyone else — knowledge, experience, keen senses of observation, fervor, honesty and conviction. Outside of medicine his knowledge was extensive in history, literature and philosophy. He carried his knowledge lightly, spicing it with homely illustration and bright anecdote. He read his lines like a fine actor, moved his audiences with oratorical splendor. Everything he said was memorable.

"Dr. Rush," Dr. David Ramsay testified, "mingled the most abstruse investigations with the most profound disquisitions." Ramsay was prosaic. Dr. Charles D. Meigs, himself a great physician, was poetic: "I was enrapt, and the spectacle of his beautiful countenance, with his earnest, most sincere, most persuasive accents, sunk so deep into my heart that neither time nor change could eradicate them from where they are at this hour freshly remembered."

Rush repaid this adoration with fatherly helpfulness. When his students went out into practice and asked for help and advice, Rush answered their questions, however paltry, in thoughtful detail. He even tried to help one lovelorn young doctor who had asked to be taught "the noble science to forget" a heartless young lady who liked to look right through the young man without seeing him.

BUT a doctor is above all a practioner, and Rush became America's most celebrated practitioner. In his best times, he was so much in demand that, when he was not in the lecture hall, he was on almost uninterrupted hospital rounds and home calls or was receiving patients in his "shop." His case records alone consumed many hours of his time. And then, on top of it all, there was his back-breaking mail-order business.

In small settlements and on isolated farms no qualified doctors were available. When home remedies failed, as they generally did, the sick mailed a description of their symptoms to a city doctor, who mailed back a prescription and named his fee, which, if he was lucky, he would sometime collect. As Rush's fame spread, his share of the mail-order practice grew enormously, even as he was having to turn away patients in Philadelphia for lack of time. He studied the symptoms with his accustomed thoroughness and mailed back recommended treatment. Many requests came from desperate, last-minute cases who would trust no one but the famous Dr. Rush.

Now, as during his apprenticeship, he continued to run across bizarre, horrifying and amusing home remedies and quack remedies. Babies with whooping cough were still being passed three times through a horse collar. Babies with croup were still wearing the right front foot of a mole tied to their necks. People with a toothache were still picking the aching tooth with the middle toe of an owl. Rush had a different cure for toothache — drops of laudanum (tincture of opium) and a blister or a "bleeding" cup behind the ear nearest the ailing tooth.

If Rush's toothache treatment seems to us almost as far-fetched as the home remedy, we must remember that all doctors were still groping in a twilight zone bordering on the midnight darkness of magic. Medicine was still in its swad-

dling clothes. Rush remembered what his preceptor, Dr.
Redman, had told him on the first chill morning of his apprenticeship: "The human body and its ailments are a hutch
of mysteries — a very few solved, the rest unsolved and perhaps insoluble."

Rush now knew from personal experience how right Redman had been. He was, therefore, humble and patient in the
presence of the unsolved and perhaps insoluble mysteries of
the human body. He knew also that if any of them were to
be solved, only painstaking, careful observation would turn
the trick. "To observe is to think," he said, "and to think
is to reason in medicine."

His sense of personal responsibility for each patient required close observation of everything that came to hand.
This meant not only observing signs and symptoms but also
successful cures — his own and those of others. Even quacks
sometimes stumbled on fragments of truth. "Converse freely
with quacks of every class and sex, such as oculists, aurists,
dentists, corn cutters, cancer doctors, etc., etc.," he advised
a young man on his way to study medicine in Europe. "You
cannot conceive how much a physician with a liberal mind
may profit from a few casual visits to these people." He himself made a collection of these remedies in what he called
his "Quack Recipe Book." If one of the recipes promised
hope of a cure, Rush used it. In the state of medical science
at the time, a doctor had to grasp at every straw.

The straws grasped at, the remedies tried in the fight
against cancer, were almost as numerous as cancer victims.
Cancer quacks had their favorite remedies. Trained doctors
had theirs. And naturally all were worthless. Rush favored
one recommended by a former student of his, Dr. Hugh Martin. Rush did not take for granted the curative virtues of
Martin's caustic powder, but subjected it to chemical tests
in the laboratory, tried it clinically on patients.

A letter from Dr. Rush to a young doctor requesting information about the treatment of a patient

Mary Washington, the President's mother, had cancer of the breast. Rush's relative, Dr. Elisha Hall, asked Rush to prescribe a remedy. He told Hall that he had used Martin's powder "in many cases with success" but that he had "failed in some." He didn't think it would help Mrs. Washington, but said Hall might "try it, diluted in water" along with other substances Rush suggested. "Under this treatment," he concluded, "she may live comfortably many years and finally die of old age." Mrs. Washington died a month later at the age of 82.

Wine and "spirits" played an important role in eighteenth-century medicine. No one with dysentery or tetanus could get well without Madeira wine and rum. Much as Rush frowned on alcohol, when his son John was two and Anne Emily was only a few months old, Rush prescribed wine for them. "A teaspoonful of old sherry every day," he wrote Julia, "will not hurt them" in damp weather.

Gout was a common disease in those days among those — it was thought — who ate and drank too generously. Rush had a treatment for this disease. If the pulse of the sufferer was "full," or "tense," he drew twelve ounces of blood. If not, he resorted to jalap, the cathartic designed for elephants, and, for good measure, five grains of calomel, a mercury purgative. Calomel not only helped to alleviate gout, it also took the enamel off the teeth!

If you were afflicted with "scales" on the face, doctors advised you to smear equal parts of tar and bees' wax on a piece of silk or leather and wear the plaster constantly until the scales came off. If this measure failed, you were advised to smear your face with white arsenic and cover it with a plaster of wax and oil. If you were still scaly after a reasonable time you were not to worry, for this was no indication that you had cancer, dropsy or consumption. You just had uncommonly stubborn scales on your face. A colleague of Rush's, Dr.

Philip Syng Physick — whose name was purely coincidental — was the same Dr. Physick who was immortalized in the following rhyme:

> Sing Physic! Sing Physic! for Philip Syng Physick
> Is dubbed Dr. Phil for his wonderful skill;
> Each sick phiz he'll physic, he'll cure every phthisic,
> Their lips fill with Physic, with potion and pill.

Dr. Physick was singled out only because of his name. All doctors' remedies were generally alike, with only a difference of emphasis here and there.

Rush was distinctly different from most doctors, however, in one important respect — his consideration for the poor. "Take care of the poor," he urged his students. "When you are called to visit a poor patient, imagine you hear a voice sounding in your ears, 'Take care of him, and I will repay thee.' " The voice was that of Boerhaave's God, who, the old Dutch doctor had said, was "the paymaster of the poor."

TODAY, under the pressure of specialization, the general practitioner is rapidly being replaced by the specialist in internal medicine. The "family doctor," with his soothing bedside manner, has virtually disappeared. Rush's bedside manner reached a new high level of compassion and tact. "In attendance upon patients," wrote Dr. David Ramsay, "Dr. Rush's manner was so gentle and sympathizing, that pain and distress were less poignant in his presence. On all occasions he exhibited the manners of a gentleman, and his conversation was sprightly, pleasant and instructive."

Even Rush's bedside manner was not left to chance. He taught his students exactly how to acquire one. He told them, for example, never to resent an affront from a sick man, never to make light of his case, never to keep him waiting, never to seem to be in a hurry, never to scribble illegible prescrip-

tions or be ignorant of their chemical composition, never to
sit on a chair but on the sick bed itself — never to wear
squeaky shoes. Above all, he said, "Let your conversation always inspire hope."

The advice was not only properly professional and humane
but good business. Rush learned from experience. "I once
lost the business of a respectable and worthy family for several years by taking up a newspaper . . . " he wrote in his
Autobiography, "and reading it while the lady of the house
was giving me an uninteresting history of the case of one of
her family."

RUSH the practitioner, the clinician, was greater than Rush
the theorizer on the cause and cure of disease. His clinical
observations, to be sure, led him to his theory — in particular
to the theory that copious bloodletting was the most effective
way to reduce an excited pulse. Bloodletting did do this. If
a dynamo had blood and enough of it were let out, the dynamo's pulse would also be reduced — to the vanishing point.

Rush's theory was wrong, but the observations on which
he based it were remarkable for their range and accuracy.
It was these observations and his untiring habit of study and
question that freed him from stale and fruitless tradition.
His habit of constantly reviewing his clinical experience
Rush owed to Dr. Thomas Sydenham. A British physician of
high standing later called him "the Sydenham of America."
That is why his contemporaries so often referred to him as
"the greatest physician" of the time, and why he continued
to be considered the greatest physician in American history
for decades after his death.

Rush's contributions to American medicine were epoch-
making. By introducing the Suttonian method of inoculation, he saved countless lives. His descriptions of yellow fever
and *cholera infantum,* his observations on diseases of the mind

and on the connection of decayed teeth with rheumatism and other diseases, his writings on tetanus, hydrophobia, croup, gout and tuberculosis — all these contain material of great value even to modern diagnosticians. He also pioneered in public medical services such as the Philadelphia Dispensary for the poor — a free dispensary with special facilities for the insane — and in preventive medicine and public sanitation.

 ## 19. From Strawberry Alley

CORNWALLIS SURRENDERED at Yorktown on October 19, 1781. The final treaty of peace, recognizing America's independence, was signed at Paris on September 3, 1783, and exactly two months later the Continental Army was formally disbanded.

Rush was still happily at war on many fronts. He was also happy at home among his growing family. Besides John and Anne Emily, called Nancy, by 1783 Julia had also borne Richard and Elizabeth, named after Mrs. Elizabeth Graeme Ferguson. Susanna, born in 1782, had died the same year. Whenever they were away at Morven with their mother, Rush sorely missed the "music" of the children's "noise." Most of all he missed Julia, who had so far outgrown "the timidity of her sex" during the war years and become "so thoroughly enlisted in the cause of her country," Rush told

John Adams, that she even "reproached" her fire-eating husband "with lukewarmness."

A mood of relaxation was general in the first postwar years — even before the final peace treaty. The task of building a strong independent America still lay ahead, but everybody, including Rush, felt the need for a little gaiety.

Not everybody, however, was as squeamish as Rush about what kind of gaiety was fitting and proper for republicans. He was as grateful to France for her timely help as anybody. But when Philadelphians completely lost their heads in celebrating the birth of a crown prince to Louis XVI in 1782, Rush, though impressed by the splendor of the celebration, was not pleased. "How great the revolution in the mind of an American!" he wrote to Mrs. Ferguson, " . . . how new the phenomenon for republicans and freemen to rejoice in the birth of a prince who must one day be the support of monarchy and slavery!"

STILL, Dr. Rush was too busy to give such lapses from republican virtue much thought, for there were many things that required doing during the postwar years. His medical practice alone kept him constantly on the jump, though his earnings from it were not high. He treated thousands of poor patients free. Other patients, including the mail-order ones, just neglected to pay. When the doctor did get paid, the pay was in rapidly depreciating Continental paper money, which became and remains a synonym for worthlessness: "It's not worth a Continental!"

"The poor are always with us." They were so much with Dr. Rush that he took to dreaming about them. He once dreamed that he had told a poor woman to find another doctor for her sick husband. She reminded the doctor of the fever that had almost killed him in 1778, and said that the prayers of his poor patients had "ascended to heaven" and saved his life. He awoke from the dream in tears, and though he didn't believe in dreams, he went back to work among the poor with renewed dedication.

As senior physician in the Pennsylvania Hospital, he often interceded to make room for free patients, but he was battling against overwhelming odds. One hospital was not enough. More hospitals and clinics were needed, and he worked out detailed plans for those he hoped would come and, largely through his efforts, finally did come. Today, as a mark of his devotion, his full-length portrait, painted by the distinguished Thomas Sully, graces the place of honor at the head of the main stairway of the original Pennsylvania Hospital building.

The first fruit of his efforts — announced on April 12, 1786 — was the opening of the Philadelphia Dispensary "for the medical relief of the poor." This first free clinic in America — and another "first" for Rush — was made possible by contributions wrung from the donors by Dr. Rush. The clinic was modest — one room in Strawberry Alley, opposite State House Square. Across the Square, in a room in the State House, Rush gave free smallpox inoculations, and went home to make red ink entries in his account book to the accompanying and compensating music of his children's noise.

PROVIDING more and better medical facilities was only one of many immediate and pressing needs. Better educational facilities was another. Rush felt that in winning the war against England, Americans had "only finished the first act of the great drama" of the Revolution. The remaining acts would have to be devoted to fighting and winning the war against potential tyranny and oppression at home. Like Thomas Jefferson, who later — in 1819 —established the University of Virginia, Rush saw education as the best insurance against these evils. Pennsylvania's one college was not adequate, even for Pennsylvania alone. More opportunity for higher education must be afforded to young men who lived far from the capital city.

The first additional opportunity came, through Rush's efforts, in the founding of a college in Carlisle, Pennsylvania, one hundred and twenty miles west of Philadelphia. It was to be a "bulwark of the blessings obtained by the Revolution," he said when he first laid plans for the college, in 1781. A necessary step in constructing this bulwark, Rush made clear to Charles Nesbit — whom he selected as first principal of the college — was political education. He said that he expected Nesbit to give "A course of lectures on government, including not only the principles of constitutions but practical legislation," which, "will be very acceptable in this country and very necessary to our republic."

Rush laid the original plans for the college, selected the principal and faculty, helped to find a site, solicited funds, secured a charter, organized the curriculum, and saw to the housing of the faculty and students. He received donations and other valuable help from John Dickinson, then President of the Council of Pennsylvania, later governor of the state. Dickinson became first President of the Board of Trustees in 1783, and the college was named after him, but Dickinson College owes its existence primarily to Benjamin Rush.

His interest in promoting education was lifelong. In 1787, he became a charter trustee of Franklin College, now Franklin and Marshall College, in Lancaster, Pennsylvania. During the next four years he wrote extensively in favor of free common schools, education for women and a national university. Like Franklin, he argued for emphasis on the study of science rather than the Greek and Latin.

Of course Rush's first love was medicine and his chief concern the advancement of medical knowledge. So when the

A letter answering an accusation "Calumnies" for Dr. Rush's part in trying to obtain a Charter for a College at Carlisle

British physician John Coakley Lettsom, whom Rush had met in London, suggested the founding of a medical society in Philadelphia, Rush eagerly approved. "The state of our country for some years past," he wrote Lettsom, "has been unfavorable to improvements of every kind in science." In 1787, Lettsom's suggestion resulted in the founding of the College of Physicians, the first American medical society. Rush was one of the twelve senior founders. Dr. John Redman became the first president. The purpose of the society, Rush told the members at an early meeting, was to exchange ideas and thereby advance medical knowledge. On his recommendation the society established a medical library, to which he and others contributed books. Today the library, second only to the Surgeon General's in Washington, is internationally famous.

Meanwhile, in article after article, Rush was making significant contributions to the medical literature of his country. Before the American Philosophical Society, after he became vice-president, he read a history of medicine in North America. He also wrote, among many other things, about a new method of curing tetanus, about the usefulness of calomel in curing the ulcerous sore throat of scarlatina (scarlet fever), about blistering and bleeding in obstinate cases of cold-weather intermittent fevers, about chemistry, veterinary science and psychiatry.

Other writings were far afield from science and medicine. They embraced arguments favoring the abolition of public oaths; arguments favoring temperance in the use of liquors and tobacco; directions for running a newspaper; counsel on manners and morals; observations on agriculture and on the conservation and wise utilization of natural resources.

These publications, together with his growing reputation as a physician and thinker, brought down on him an avalanche of letters requesting advice on forestry and penology, on the ventilation of ships and the training of children, on the liberation of the Spanish provinces in South America and the origin of prehistoric mounds in Ohio. In the small hours of the morning he answered the letters patiently and wisely.

MANY of these interests could only be fringe interests. One other — in addition to medicine, science, education and government — was close to his heart. This was Negro slavery, the greatest of American sins. Rush, one of the earliest Abolitionists, was familiar with slavery. Pennsylvanians owned slaves, and Rush's father had been a slave owner.

No matter how well treated a slave might be, slavery had to go, Rush said, for it was "an hydra sin, a vice which degrades human nature." He denounced its injustice and cruelty, the unpunished crimes against slaves, including murder. The thievery and laziness attributed to slaves by their owners, he said, was the fault of the owners themselves. Only slave traders and slave owners could be blamed for the heartless breaking up of Negro families — first in Africa, then in America — and in particular for the crime of selling parents and children to different owners.

Slavery, Rush said, was not only a sin but an unnecessary one. Crops could be grown without slave labor. He advised teaching Negroes reading and writing, training them in useful occupations as preparation for emancipation. He proposed an immediate boycott against importers of slaves and against shipowners who brought them to this country, also laws to limit present servitude and a high duty on incoming slaves.

Back before the war, Rush, aided by James Pemberton, a Quaker merchant and philanthropist, had aroused enough sympathy among Philadelphians to enable him to found the first anti-slavery society in America. The war interrupted the work of this Pennsylvania Society for Promoting the Abolition of Slavery in America. After the war, in 1787, the Society came to life again and gained new members. Benjamin Franklin was elected president, Rush secretary. The Society's work went on. In 1803, Rush was elected president.

Rush was a practical man. That is why he became a gunpowder expert early in the war, and why he became a maple sugar expert now. He learned all about maple trees — their growth and distribution, how to tap them and how to make maple sugar in Pennsylvania, which imported cane sugar from the West Indies. The maple sugar business, he said, would be "the happy means of rendering the commerce and slavery of our African brethren, in the sugar Islands as unnecessary, as it has always been inhuman and unjust."

NEGRO slaves were not the only ones to suffer cruel punishments, which Rush condemned no matter who the victims were. In his day, authorities did not try too hard to make the punishment fit the crime — or misdemeanor. Even minor offenders were punished publicly at the whipping post or in the stocks or pillory. A public whipping, a public hanging drew crowds of idle sadists.

Again Rush was the first to propose reform. In "An Enquiry into the Effects of Public Punishments upon Criminals, and upon Society" he argued that "a man who has lost his character at a whipping-post, has nothing valuable left to lose in society." This and other harsh punishment, he said, destroyed human dignity, and served only to harden the criminal, corrupt the punisher and encourage further crime. Prisons should employ humane treatment to restore the erring to useful citizenship. A jail should have a place of worship, a garden and a workshop. The prisoner should be taught a trade and be paid for his work. Bodily pain, exile, forced labor and solitary confinement only defeated their own ends. Though far in advance of the time, these ideas led to significant reforms in Pennsylvania and other states.

So also did his campaign against indiscriminate capital punishment. At the time, burglars and robbers as well as murderers often suffered the death penalty. This was unjust, Rush contended. Besides, he said, by no means are *all* murders cold-blooded and deliberate. Most murders result from "a sudden gust of passion." A distinction should be made between such murders and those that were the result of "a malignity of heart." But even hanging a cold-blooded murderer is folly, since "Murder is propagated by hanging for murder." In his own lifetime Rush's arguments bore fruit. In 1794, the penal code of Pennsylvania was revised and, except for first-degree murder, the death penalty was abolished. The reform was not all Rush's doing, but he deserves major credit.

THE ten years or so immediately after the war were perhaps the most fruitful of Rush's life. During the hectic postwar years, he left indelible marks on America's medical, educational and social institutions. While doing so, he found time to help shape the political form of the new nation, by acting as a delegate to the Pennsylvania Convention that ratified the Federal Constitution at the end of 1787.

But battle takes its toll, and Rush found that his numerous victories were not enough to compensate for the enmity and opposition he had aroused. He felt them deeply. By 1789, he had decided to retire from the battlefield. He "took leave of public life . . . for ever." he hoped, and begged his sons never to enter it — "beyond a vote at an election." He urged them "rather to be soldiers than politicians, should they ever be so unfortunate as to live in a country distracted by a civil war. In battle men kill, without hating each other; in political contests men hate without killing, but in that hatred they commit murder every hour of their lives."

On December 29, 1789 — five days after his forty-fourth birthday — he wrote to Noah Webster, author of the Dictionary, that he now "expected to live only for the benefit of my family and my patients." But almost as he wrote these words the most violent storm of his life was forming thunderheads on the horizon.

 20. Yellow Fever

AFTER THE BIRTH of the new American nation, life in Philadelphia for the well-to-do was one of health, happiness and economic boom. Among society folk, the jubilant mood that marked the unrepublican celebration of the birth of the French Dauphin in 1782 grew into a settled habit that present-day advertisers of luxury goods would call gracious living. Rich women bought imported British finery with a lavish hand and showed it off in their shiny coaches and "chairs." They and their sporty husbands, brothers and sweethearts lived on a lavish scale. They had helped to defeat the mightiest kingdom on earth, and felt that they had earned the right to dress as well and step as high as any court in Europe. It was unrepublican perhaps — but what of it?

Old Quakers knew the answer: the Lord would have vengeance. Partly because of his Quaker heritage, partly because he was republican to the bone, partly because he pitied and honored the poor, Dr. Rush disapproved strongly of all the expansiveness, conspicuous waste and dram-drinking. Workmen — and the slightly higher economic orders — couldn't share in the gracious living, couldn't even pay their doctors' bills. High living began only in the higher reaches of the middle class.

Dr. Rush — gunsmith's and small shopkeeper's son — couldn't stomach the high-stepping "aristocracy." One aristocratic gentleman in particular, Rush believed with Secretary of State Thomas Jefferson, had compounded the calamitous condition of the poor and nearly ruined the country. This gentleman was Alexander Hamilton, Washington's Secretary of the Treasury. It was the "brilliant boy" Hamilton who master-minded the passage of the cynical Funding Bill of 1790. He was the intellectual leader of the Federalists and a confirmed enemy of democracy and republicanism. "The people!" he said, " — the people is a great beast!"

His Funding Bill was calculated to make the rich richer and the poor poorer. During the war the government had piled up a mountainous debt. It owed soldiers their long-overdue back pay and mustering-out pay. To other citizens it owed money borrowed from them, and money for quartermaster supplies bought from them on credit. All these debts had been paid in "certificates" — that is, in government I.O.U.'s to be redeemed at some time in the future. To the holder it looked as if it would be a long time before their I.O.U.'s could be redeemed at face value. When the holders became hard-pressed for cash to buy necessities, they were forced to sell their certificates for whatever they could get, which became less and less with every passing month. The rich bought them up at ever-dwindling prices. Many con-

gressmen had bought certificates, and were not likely to oppose legislation that would enable the government to redeem
them.

Hamilton's Funding Bill was bitterly opposed by Jefferson, by James Madison and, from the political sidelines, by
Benjamin Rush. When it came to a vote in Congress, however, it passed — along with the tax legislation necessary to
make the now-valuable certificates eventually redeemable by
the government. Unfortunately, the tax money would have
to come in large part from the very people who had sold their
certificates to buy necessities.

The effect of the Funding Bill was disastrous to all but the
speculators. Bankruptcies and suicides became daily occur-
rences. Men wept in the streets, brawled in the coffee houses.
The national economy, with its lifeblood — money — drained off into certificate-speculation, reeled and collapsed. The
old Quakers, who had prophesied that the Lord would have
vengeance, now saw the prophesy being fulfilled. The old
Quakers didn't know it, but there was a greater tragedy still
in store for Philadelphia.

MEANWHILE, Dr. Rush went on working himself into another
collapse. When he recovered, he moved his growing family
into a larger house at 83 Walnut Street. This was in 1791.
Julia had just given birth to their tenth child, Benjamin.
Four of the children had died. Besides Benjamin, then, they
now had John, 14, Anne Emily, 12, Richard, 11, Mary, 7, and
James, 5.

However busy and exhausted, the doctor spent nineteen
out of twenty evenings with the children and Julia, "friend
... companion ... wife." To the boys he devoted "a great
deal of time." John, the oldest, he was introducing to the
"painful and bloody" mysteries of medicine. Once, in 1792,
he took Julia and the girls "to see a male Lyon 25 months

old in Race Street." It was a happy and frivolous interlude in the midst of one tragedy and preceding another.

For Julia the interlude must have been especially welcome. She was not only the manager of a populous and noisy household, but also the children's principal teacher. Her husband believed that an educated father should be responsible for the education of young children, but his practice and many other affairs forced him to leave most of their education to his "prudent and sensible wife." Even when the boys were taken off Julia's hands, as they went off to school and then to college, she always had three of the doctor's hungry and obstreperous apprentices boarding with the family. Often, also, Rush's mother, Susanna, and sister Rebecca added to the family traffic, to say nothing of the many visitors who came and stayed for days at a time. Through it all the capable Julia remained calm, cool and serene.

While affairs in Philadelphia were generally in a bad way, Rush was gratified by the realization of two projects close to his heart. In the spring of 1792, the state Assembly appropriated £15,000 (The American dollar, officially adopted by Congress in 1785, was minted for the first time the same year as the Assembly's appropriation — 1792.) to build a separate house for the insane at the Pennsylvania Hospital. At the same session the Assembly established free schools. "I mention this," Rush wrote, "to encourage my boys to expect great things from slender beginnings and weak instruments."

In late summer, 1793, while Philadelphia was still deep in economic crisis, a greater tragedy struck the city. The first signs were not alarming. As always at this time of year people were coming down with fevers. On August 4, Polly Bradford, Tom Bradford's wife, developed symptoms of bilious remittent fever. These were pains in the back and head, full pulse, inflamed eyes tinged with yellow, vomiting, cold hands and feet, and a searing pain in the liver. Rush sent her to bed and ordered two bleedings and a dose of calomel (a mercury medicine) . She recovered. On August 5, Rush heard that the young daughter of Dr. Hugh Hodge was ill with a bilious fever. She died on August 7. Dr. Hodge did not believe in bleeding. Did that explain the child's death? Perhaps. And yet —

On the same day that Rush had prescribed for Polly Bradford he had bled and purged a young Mr. McNair, who also had symptoms of a bilious fever. He died a week later. That made one success, one failure.

On August 19, Dr. Hodge and Dr. John Foulke, one of Rush's former students, called Rush into consultation at the bedside of Mrs. Peter LeMaigre, who lived on Water Street, a hundred yards from the river wharves. Mrs. LeMaigre was suffering from constant vomiting and a painful burning sensation in the stomach. The three doctors could see that she was dying from bilious fever. They stepped into an adjoining room. As they did so, a pattern of evidence began forming in Rush's mind.

"I have seen an unusual number of fevers much like this one," he said. "The symptoms are uncommonly malignant. I wonder — "

"So have I," Hodge interrupted. "Several persons near here, including my daughter, have died of similar fevers."

"I wonder why so many deaths have occurred in this particular neighborhood," Rush said, frowning.

"This probably has nothing to do with it," Foulke said, "but you must have noticed the stench in the air as you came here, sir."

"Yes, I did. What causes it?"

"Large mounds of rotting coffee on Ball's wharf and the one next to it. Do you suppose, sir—"

Rush snapped his fingers. He turned to Hodge. "You live only a few doors from here, Doctor, and your daughter died of the fever. A patient of mine, Mrs. Bradford, spent an afternoon near these wharves just before falling ill of the fever. Her sister, Mrs. Leaming, visited her there that afternoon, and also came down with the fever. I bled and purged both of them, and —"

"Humph!" went Hodge. "You and your bleeding!"

"They both recovered!" Rush snapped. "But I am not just now defending my methods, sir. I am only struck that so many fever cases have appeared in this neighborhood — near the putrifying coffee. Another patient of mine, Mr. McNair, worked several days near Ball's wharf before he took the fever. I remember now, Dr. Foulke, that he complained of the smell."

"I know about your Mr. McNair," Hodge growled. "You bled him and purged him and he died."

"I am not saying that I could have saved your daughter with my treatment, Dr. Hodge," Rush said. "But I am now convinced that the putrid exhalations from that coffee started this epidemic."

"Epidemic! Nonsense, sir!"

"Yes, epidemic," Rush said. "But I do not believe the coffee is the direct cause of all the cases. The fever has spread too far from here to believe that. The fever is clearly contagious. One catches it from another."

"So now it's contagion!" Hodge sneered.

"Contagion, yes. We experienced the same contagious fever in '62."

"When you were an apprentice not yet dry behind the ears."

Rush started for the street door. "I am dry behind the ears now, Doctor, and I say we have a contagious epidemic fever on our hands."

Dr. Hodge and Dr. Foulke went back into the sickroom. Dr. Rush softly closed the street door behind him, paused a moment on the stoop and sniffed at the putrid air.

Mrs. LeMaigre died the next day.

As Rush walked away from the LeMaigre house, he thanked God that Julia, the girls and the two youngest boys were safe at Morven for the summer. John and Richard, however, were still with him in town. As the days passed, the fever spread farther and farther from what Rush considered the original source of infection, the rotting coffee.

"The disease is violent and of short duration," he wrote to Julia. No medication seemed effective. Deaths mounted. "You can recollect," he wrote again, "how much the loss of a single patient once in a month used to affect me. Judge then how I must feel in hearing every morning of the death of three or four!" The schools were either closed or deserted, he informed Julia in another letter, and he was afraid John and Richard would be infected from his clothes. He was, therefore, sending them to Morven, along with a copy of Paley's *Moral Philosophy*. "It will qualify you above all things to educate our children properly." He urged her to keep their noses to the grindstone.

The College of Physicians met in emergency session. It appointed a committee to draft instructions for the people of the stricken city. The committee proved unnecessary: Rush had instructions all ready. He recommended that all houses with yellow fever cases be marked, sick rooms be kept clean and well aired. It would be one hundred and seven years before Dr. Walter Reed proved what Rush could not know — that keeping a yellow fever victim's room or house well aired was the surest way of guaranteeing that the disease-carryed *Aëdes aegypti* mosquito would get in, bite the victim and carry the fever to others.

Rush also advised that hot sun, fatigue and spirituous liquors should be avoided, that daily disinfection should be carried out with burning gunpowder, vinegar and camphor. A hospital for the poor, he said, was sorely needed. And the mournful tolling of funeral bells must be stopped. It only encouraged panic.

There was panic enough already. Rush and those who agreed with him said that the villain of the piece was a "noxious miasma" rising from all rotting matter, from stagnant pools and swamps, from the mouths of the fever-ridden. The miasma, then, must be burned away. Good. People lighted fires on every street corner. Rush and other doctors warned that the fires were dangerous and probably useless. It would be better to burn gunpowder. Good. The miasma-fighters now unlimbered their muskets and blazed away at the miasma from their windows. The musket-fire riddled the miasma fruitlessly, and it also riddled Philadelphians. The mayor ordered a cease-fire.

Many doctors did not agree with Rush's "noxious miasma" theory on the origin of the fever. For them his theory was disloyal to the city. It made the origin shamefully local. It was bad for business and ruined real estate values. They preferred to think the fever had been imported from the West Indies by foreigners and sailors.

If Rush was right, his sanitation program — a general cleaning up of the city, the drying up of stagnant pools, the draining of swamps — was the answer. If his opponents were right, quarantine of incoming ships would at least prevent more infection from entering the city. We now know that some truth lay on both sides. Originally the fever had indeed been imported, but the infection was spread by mosquitoes, which bred in the Philadelphia pools and swamps.

It soon became clear that Rush was right about one thing:

there *was* a fever epidemic. The prime question was how to
cure the fever. "The common remedies for malignant fevers
have all failed," Rush wrote Julia. The purges he prescribed
at first were ineffectual, so he tried various barks, wine,
brandy and aromatics. They didn't work either. Blistering
the limbs, neck and head was equally unsuccessful. Wrap-
ping the entire body in blankets dipped in vinegar and rubbing the patient's sides with a mercurial ointment to stimu-
late the liver and thereby the whole system left the fever un-
touched. Three out of every four of his fever patients died.
Dr. Edward Stevens from St. Croix in the West Indies was
in Philadelphia. Perhaps he could help. Rush called on him.
Stevens advised throwing buckets of cold water on his patients. Rush tried it the next day. Three out of four who
suffered this brisk treatment died.

Then one August night, among some old documents, he
found a paper written in 1744 by Dr. John Mitchell. It de-
scribed the yellow fever epidemics in Virginia a half century before. Rush thumbed anxiously through the pages.
What cure did Mitchell recommend? Here it was: Mitchell
wrote that "evacuation by purges was more necessary in this
than in most other fevers, and that an ill-timed scrupulous-
ness about the weakness of the body was of bad consequence
in these urging circumstances." Mitchell reported that he
had purged yellow fever patients when the pulse was so weak
it could hardly be felt. The patients had recovered. Rush
stopped to think . . . . What purge would be best?

He remembered that during the Revolution he had seen
Dr. Thomas Young use ten grains of calomel combined with
ten grains of jalap, the "elephant's cathartic." The combination had come to be known as "ten and ten." After much
soul-searching, Rush decided to try it, but often increased the
jalap dose to fifteen grains. It seemed to work so well that he
buttonholed his colleagues on the street and urged them to

follow his example. If the pulse was full or tense after this grandiose purge, he advised taking eight to ten ounces of blood. Of course a proper diet was necessary — tea, chicken broth and other liquids, fruit, and bland foods such as gruel, tapioca and sago.

Some doctors had fled from the city, but most of those who remained rejected Rush's treatment. His bleeding and purging, they said, were taking many lives. On September 12, in an open letter to the College of Physicians published in the *Federal Gazette*, Rush entered a public defense. "I have bled twice in many, and in one acute case, four times, with the happiest effects," he wrote. "I consider intrepidity in the use of the lancet at present to be as necessary, as it is in the use of mercury and jalap, in this insidious and ferocious disease."

Five days later, also in the *Federal Gazette*, Dr. William Currie attacked Rush for his bloodletting. Currie didn't even believe there was any yellow fever in the city. Rush replied the next day. He himself, he said, had just had yellow fever and had been cured by two generous bleedings and two doses of mercury in two days. Evidently Rush's intrepidity in practice was getting exceptionally good results — good enough, at least, to convince Currie. On October 2, he admitted that bloodletting and purging were proper remedies, and said that most physicians now agreed with Rush. But a minority of doctors continued their vendetta against him.

An October cold-snap accomplished what bloodletting, calomel and jalap couldn't possibly accomplish. It killed the mosquitoes that had been spreading the fever. Rush's all-noticing eye had observed the unusually numerous mosquitoes that had been spreading the fever, but neither he nor anyone else had attached any significance to them.

After the cold weather began, the number of fever patients declined. In November and December there were only a few

new cases. The epidemic was over, and on December 12, the
whole state celebrated a special thanksgiving. But the yellow
fever of 1793 had taken a toll of nearly one-tenth of the city's
population. The old Quakers' Lord had had his vengeance.

> Doctors raving and disputing,
> Death's pale army still recruiting
>   What a pother,
>   One with 'tother,
> Some a-writing, some a-shooting.

> Nature's poisons here collected,
> Water, earth and air infected;
> O' what pity
>   Such a city
> Was in such a place erected.

By the end of 1793 "Death's pale army" had practically
stopped recruiting among fever patients, but the doctors had
not stopped disputing about the origin and proper treatment of the disease. Then when a few cases appeared in the
spring and early summer of 1794, the disputants stepped up
the debate, and apprehensive talk began again in the taverns
and market places.

Toward the end of August, Rush, in an address before
the State Committee of Health, warned that the filthy water
in the city's countless stagnant pools and gutters was connected with yellow fever. To prevent the fever from spreading as it had in 1793, he urged a general cleanup. Rush was
at once attacked in an anonymous letter to the *Gazette of the
United States*. The writer rightly insisted that the fever was
not contagious, but out of misguided municipal loyalty he
maintained that the fever was not yellow fever. To make
either claim, he said, would only upset the citizens and dis-
rupt business.

There was more to this attack on Rush than appeared on the surface. The *Gazette* was edited by John Ward Fenno, a protégé of Alexander Hamilton. It was constructive and strongly Federalist. It was critical of Jefferson, leader in the struggle for democratic rights. It was pro-British and anti-French. It had defended speculation in certificates and supported Hamilton's Funding Bill. And it knew that on all these matters, Rush stood on what the *Gazette* considered the wrong side. It was willing to print an attack on him as much because he was a Jeffersonian as because he insisted that the fever was yellow fever and that it was of local origin.

A letter by Rush to the Committee of Health on the danger of the views expressed in the letter to the *Gazette* had no effect. The committee agreed with the anonymous letter-writer.

The fever spread, and Rush went on prescribing practically the same remedies as he had used the year before. Bleeding and purging continued to be the mainstays of his treatment. On November 4, 1794, he reported that "Out of upwards of 120 'strongly marked' cases, I lost but two where my prescriptions were followed on the first day of the disorder."

He believed later that his success in the treatment of yellow fever was the greatest in his thirty-four years of practice. At the time of his success, however, he was accused of bleeding patients to death. Some said he was nothing but a horse doctor. Some said he was insane. Some wished to drive him out of the city.

Fortunately, the disease was less virulent than in 1793, and there were far fewer cases. By the time winter came, the city's health was normal. At last Rush had time to consider measures for preventing future epidemics. In addition to his cleanup campaign, he proposed quarantine and the placing of barriers across streets struck by the fever. Only doctors and nurses, he said, should be allowed in the infected streets and houses. Healthy persons should be moved out of them at public expense and domiciled in tents or other temporary dwellings. Nothing came of his suggestions, most of which would have been of little avail in any event.

In the summer of 1795, there were only isolated cases of yellow fever, a fact that Rush attributed to the heavy rains and cool weather. During this summer, also, Rush's mother, Susanna, died. She was buried beside her first husband, John, in Christ Church Yard. A month later Julia bore her twelfth child, Samuel.

The year 1796 was also a healthy one. The debate over the origin and treatment of yellow fever was still going on, but in less strident tones. Rush was still convinced that the disease was of local origin, and he was pleased to know — and to let others know — that physicians in Baltimore and New York agreed with him. In 1796, it probably seemed to many that the point was hardly worth emphasizing. But soon — too soon — the graveyards would be filling again and Rush's point at least worth debating.

21. Libel

THE YEAR 1797 was another bad yellow fever year, not only for Philadelphia, the fever's special target, but for New York and Boston as well. Every Philadelphian who could afford it, fled the city. Thousands camped in tents on the outskirts, where, chances were, the Aëdes mosquito also camped.

In the city itself, the theaters, taverns, coffee houses and dance halls were closed. Hospital carts and hearses rumbled through the all-but-empty streets. Their drivers, stopping to breathe their horses, could hear only the coffin-makers' hammers, the groans of the sick and dying, the sobbing of mourners.

Many doctors, forgetting their Hippocratic oath, ran for their lives. But Dr. Benjamin Rush, the much-reviled, stuck to his oath and to the city of death. His theory about the cause of the disease, and his treatments were basically wrong, but his heart was in the right place. His motives and courage were beyond question, even by most of his worst enemies. The quality of his courage shows in the reply he made to Julia when she begged him not to expose himself "a second time to the dangers and distresses of the year 1793." He answered: "If I thought by remaining in the city, I should *certainly die,* I should think it my duty to stay. I will not quit my post."

Nor, despite vitriolic criticism, would he abandon his method of cure, as grateful patients testified. But the voices of his patients were lost in the torrent of abuse directed at the overworked and sensitive Rush. Toward the end of the epidemic, he wrote John Dickinson that "Such seasons as we have just witnessed are called 'the doctors' harvests.' To me it has been a harvest, but it has been of unprofitable labor, anxious days, sleepless nights, and a full and overflowing measure of the most merciless persecution. I have not merited the indifference with which the citizens of Philadelphia have witnessed the butchery of my character."

One of the busiest of the "butchers" was the arch-Federalist John Ward Fenno, who, in 1793, had published the anonymous attack on Rush in his *Gazette of the United States.* His attacks on Rush's character and motives and on what he called Rush's "lunatic system" of medicine were unremitting. At length the doctor's raw nerves could stand no more. He brought suit for libel. Fenno's defense is clear from the title of an article — "Assault on the Liberty of the Press" — that appeared in the *Gazette* on October 3, 1797. The suit did not progress beyond its initial stages, but not because of the validity of Fenno's defense. Libel suits against American citizens were rarely successful in American courts. This was probably in part why Rush dropped the suit. But there was another reason.

FENNO had found an able ally in his political crusade against

Dr. Benjamin Rush aiding sufferers in the Yellow Fever Plague of 1793

Jefferson and in his politico-medical crusade against Rush. This was William Cobbett, an English writer and politician who had come to the United States in 1792 and to Philadelphia in 1794. By 1797, he had endeared himself to the Federalists, such as Hamilton and Fenno, by his cleverly satirical and abusive attacks in the newspapers on anyone who disagreed with his Royalist-Federalist politics. "Cobbett," writes the editor of Rush's *Letters*, "was one of the most colorful figures in his own era, and in his genius for savage journalistic satire remains perhaps without a rival in any era."

This is a restrained characterization. Another writer — referring to the first appearance of Cobbett's *Porcupine's Gazette* in March, 1797 — says that "A new Knight of Scurrility had entered the lists, encouraged by Hamilton, armed with a pen that flowed poison. He had previously distinguished himself by his brilliant and abusive pamphlets attacking [Joseph] Priestley (the liberal minister and discoverer of oxygen, who was forced to leave England because of his sympathy with the French Revolution; Dr. Rush had sold Priestley a small parcel of land west of Philadelphia on which he made his home), the Democratic Societies, and the Irish, and by his exhibition in his shop window of pictures of George III and Lord North, with Franklin and Sam Adams coupled with fools and knaves. His unlimited capacity for abuse, his insane fury against the French Revolution, his unfathomable contempt for democracy, his devotion to England, fitted in with the spirit of society." That is, high Tory society.

Many, including Abigail Adams, the President's wife, admired the wit and humor of Cobbett, or "Peter Porcupine," as he signed himself. The Tories, the Federalists — the rich, the well-born and the fashionable — were his natural allies. They loved him. Others — such as Jefferson, David Rittenhouse, Sam Adams, Tom Paine and Benjamin Rush, whom Cobbett called "French Democrats" — were his natural enemies.

Part of the deed of transference of property by Dr. Rush to Joseph Priestley — English chemist who escaped to America

Rush, the uncompromising — whom Cobbett labeled a "poisonous trans-Atlantic quack" — for both political and medical reasons was an invitingly obvious target. In 1793, Rush had resigned from the College of Physicians because his disagreement with its members could not be reconciled, and now, in 1797, he was fighting the College again. Together with friends on the faculty of the University, he organized an opposition society, the Academy of Medicine. Its short life was spent in trying to prove the local origin of yellow fever. It campaigned in vain for a cleanup of streets, gutters, ponds and marshes. Those opposed to the Academy reserved most of their fire for its leader, Rush.

Cobbett set the scurrilous tone and style for the abuse. As a mild example of how low Cobbett could get, consider his account in one issue of his Journal of Rush's behavior four years earlier: "So much was the Doctor . . . possessed with the notion that he was the only man of common sense existing, that he not only refused to consult with any but his former pupils who submitted to obey his dictates, and rudely intruded his advice upon other people's patients. He also appointed two illiterate Negro men, and sent them into all the alleys and bye places in the city, with orders to bleed, and give his sweating purges . . . to all they should find sick . . . and bloody and dirty work they made among the poor miserable creatures that fell in their way."

Cobbett's harking back over four years to 1793 reflects the continuity of the persecution. "Ever since the year 1793," Rush wrote to a former student, Dr. John R. B. Rodgers, of the Columbia Medical College in New York, "I have lived in Philadelphia as in a foreign country." He felt deserted by his friends and surrounded by enemies. His practice was nearly ruined. Therefore, he told Rodgers, he had determined to move to New York if there was a professorship open at Columbia. Rodgers and others on the Columbia medical

William Cobbett

faculty were delighted by the prospect of securing the services of the distinguished Philadelphia physician and medical scientist.

On October 20, 1797, the medical faculty voted unanimously in Rush's favor. His presence, they said, would be in the best interests of the Medical College and would enhance the reputation of Columbia College as a whole. It only remained to get the approval of the Board of Trustees. Here was the rub. The "brilliant boy" Federalist, Alexander Hamilton, was a trustee. He was opposed to appointing a republican physician however distinguished, and Rush did not receive the appointment.

Rodgers proposed that Rush come to New York and give a course of lectures. Disappointed and shocked, Rush decided against the proposal. He then thought of moving to the country and becoming a farmer. But his funds were small and his family large. The dream of farming would have to remain unfulfilled. The old warrior, now nearly fifty-two, would stay in Philadelphia and carry on the fight as best he could.

But while he fought on, what would his family eat? Two years earlier he had declined the directorship of the United States Mint because he was devoted to his profession. Now, in 1797, President John Adams, his old friend and admirer, came to the rescue. Rush knew that the post was still open. The salary was $1,200 a year and the duties light enough not to interfere with his dwindled practice. Indirectly he let Adams know that he would be glad to accept the appointment. There were some forty other applicants, but after carefully reviewing their qualifications, Adams selected Rush, who held the position until his death.

The salary, added to what fees he was still collecting, took care of his economic problem tolerably well. But he had other worries. The more his few remaining friends defended him in letters to the newspapers, the more violent became the at-

Dr. Benjamin Rush, portrait by Thomas Sully

tacks of Fenno and Cobbett. He had dropped his suit against
Fenno but in December, 1797, Rush brought suit for libel
against Cobbett in the Supreme Court of Pennsylvania. Because the defendant was a British subject and because the
amount being sued for was in excess of $500, Cobbett re-
quested that the case be tried before the United States Cir-
cuit Court. After some delay the request was denied in March,
1798. Several postponements followed, but at last in December, 1799, the case came to trial before the Pennsylvania Supreme Court. The verdict was in favor of Rush. He was
awarded $5,000 damages, and Cobbett was also obliged to
pay legal costs of $3,000.

The fretful "Porcupine" was determined to get revenge.
He wrote to a friend in the British legation: "Nothing pro-
vokes me but the thought of such a whining republican ras-
cal putting the 5,000 dollars in his pocket. Why, the pauper
never saw so much money before, not even in his *mint* . . .
The villain shall not enjoy his prize in peace."

Cobbett lost no time. He closed down his *Porcupine's
Gazette,* moved to New York and started *The Rush-Light,*
"By the help of which, Wayward and Disaffected Britons may
see a Complete Specimen of the Baseness, Dishonesty, Ingratitude, and Perfidy of Republicans, and of the Profligacy,
Injustice, and Tyranny of Republican Government." On the
title page he let it be known that the new publication was
written by the same winsome "Peter Porcupine" whose venom had dripped from the pages of his *Gazette.* This was a
promise that more venom was to come.

In the first issue, dated February 15, 1800, the author assured the public that in *The Rush-Light* it would "be able
to see a good many very pretty things." He began by identi-
fying "The loathsome, subject, now before me," as "Doctor
Benjamin Rush, the noted bleeding physician of Philadelphia." Later in the same issue he called Rush "the Pennsyl-

vanian *Hippocrates*," an "insinuating" hypocrite, a thorough ignoramus. He charged that Rush was "the intimate of *Jefferson*," which, unfortunately, Rush was not, and that he was full "of the politicks of Tom Paine," which he was.

Cobbett did not train his "Light" on Rush alone. His vilification embraced the whole family, whose members, he said, were "objects of as perfect insignificance as is the poverty-bred plant, the name of which he bears, and the worthlessness of which is proverbial." He sneered at Rush's father because he had been a blacksmith. He accused Susanna, Rush's mother of having run a kind of speakeasy in her shop. He attacked Rush's sons, with some truth, for a youthfully extravagant reprisal and for a reprisal against their father's slanderers, among whom Cobbett had achieved first rank.

During its brief life *The Rush-Light* was a smash hit. It sold fabulously, and Cobbett had visions of making a $10,000 profit out of it. Almost overnight it snatched away the victory Rush had won in the libel suit. Rush's family became anxious and distressed — almost maddened. Richard, now twenty, "assaulted" a Dr. Glentworth for what the family considered a lie Cobbett had reported. John, now twenty-three, took the stage for New York to challenge Cobbett to a duel, which fortunately did not take place. The schoolmates of the younger children made them miserable by poking savage fun at them.

But the publication's day of lush infamy was short. The fifth number of *The Rush-Light*, published in April, 1800, was the last. Cobbett had run out of poison. He was also faced with exposure and trial as a British agent. Afraid that he could not win this case either and that he would be forcibly deported, he sailed for England on June 1. He had not paid the $8,000 judgment against him, but it was eventually settled through his lawyers for about half the amount. Rush donated his share to charity.

Philip Freneau, the Jeffersonian poet, bade him *bon voyage:*

> O may the sharks enjoy their bait:
> He came such mischief to create
> We wish him not a better fate.

Cobbett was defeated and gone, but as many of Rush's friends had foretold, the clever libeler had made almost a shambles of the great doctor's reputation. Many physicians and laymen alike were inclined to think him a mere medical fanatic. All of the failures of bloodletting — a practice common before his time and for more than a century afterwards — they tended to lay exclusively at his door. Even some modern historians, overlooking his many epoch-making contributions to American medicine, have dismissed him with an easy phrase — "wielder of the lancet."

He was far more than that. If he had been heeded during the yellow fever years, if Philadelphia had been cleaned up and its many mosquito-breeding waters had been drained and its open cisterns covered, much illness and death would have been prevented. Of course, neither Rush nor anyone else at the time could possibly have guessed the real reason for the effectiveness of such measures, but the fact remains that Rush's hunch about stagnant waters and swamps was right.

He was so often right in his hunches, so sharp an observer, that his convictions were always based on the facts as he saw them — and no one else saw so many facts or saw them so clearly. When new facts proved an old view wrong, he gave it up at once, which is all that can be expected of a scientist. When his observations proved that yellow fever was not contagious, for example, he abandoned the contagion theory. But there was nothing to prove that yellow fever was not of local origin, and much to indicate that it was. His local-origin

Residence of Dr. Benjamin Rush, at the time of his death, 98 South 4th Street, Philadelphia

theory was a good working hypothesis, and he was right in sticking to it until facts proved it untenable.

WITH the turn of the century, life became quieter and happier for the old physician. The epidemics declined in severity. As they did so, the vendetta against him became less bitter. The unpopularity of his political views also declined after Jefferson was elected President in 1800, and the struggle between Federalists and Democrats subsided.

Rush withdrew from active political life and devoted himself to health and welfare. In the relative calm of the new times he found the leisure to begin writing his autobiography, which he called *Travels Through Life*. But his deep concern for the sick and especially for the mentally ill — in his day the neglected and brutally treated discards of society — led him into still other uncharted seas. His former travels he was recording in the past tense, but he was living his new travels in the present.

22. Father of American Psychiatry

On November 4, 1812, five and a half months before his death, Rush wrote to John Adams about a book of his that had just been published:

> "Herewith you will receive a copy of my *Medical Inquiries and Observations upon Diseases of the Mind.* I shall wait with solicitude to receive your opinion of them ... The subjects of them have hitherto been enveloped in mystery. I have endeavored to bring them down to the level of all the other diseases of the human body, and to show that the mind and body are moved by the same causes and subject to the same laws. For this attempt to simplify the "medicina mentis" [medicine of the mind] I expect no quarter from my learned brethren. But time I hope will do my opinions justice."

Adams and other members of the legal profession liked the book and said so. When asked, Jefferson said he would welcome a copy. "I read with delight everything which comes from your pen," he wrote, "and the subject of this work is peculiarly interesting." But Rush's "learned brethren," the physicians, stood mute.

Time, as Rush hoped, did the book justice. Before its appearance no book of its kind existed, and for nearly a century after its appearance, American medical schools could not find a better one in the field. It was another "first" for Rush and, like his *Directions for Preserving the Health of Soldiers,* another classic.

TRAGIC irony shadows Rush's interest in mental illness, an interest that began many years before he succeeded in creating an insane ward in the Pennsylvania Hospital — the very ward in which his son John was placed in 1810. The irony is compounded by the pride Rush took in young John's interest in a mad woman when, one day, the nine-year-old boy was accompanying his father on his hospital rounds. As they walked away from the hospital, John asked many troubled questions about madness. Two of them Rush was to spend the rest of his life trying to answer: How do people go mad? Is it possible to cure madness?

Until Rush's time the two favorite explanations of the causes of madness were that it was the work of the devil or that the insane were suffering for their sins. Rush was the first American to propose that mental illness was a disease, not a devilish "possession" or a punishment for sin.

But exactly what kind of disease was it? What was its pathology? By 1795, after careful observation and thought, Rush had a theory. He then wrote to Dr. John Redman Coxe, Rush's former apprentice and grandson of Dr. John Redman. "I have lately adopted a new theory of mania," he said.

"I suppose it in nearly all cases to be accompanied by inflammation in the brain." Some writers have accused Rush of arriving at his theories through pure reason. It is true that he did arrive at some of his theories in this way, but his theory of mania did not rest only on pure reason. He told Coxe that the changes in the brains of insane patients observed at autopsy resembled those in other diseased parts of the body.

By the time his great book on diseases of the mind appeared in 1812, he was able to specify what he considered the cause of the brain inflammation found at autopsy. The main cause of insanity, he said, was "disordered actions" in the blood vessels of the brain, as in other "arterial diseases." This view anticipated the modern idea that many types of mental illness are due to disordered brain circulation.

But there were other physical causes of insanity, he believed. These were overexposure to extremes of heat or cold, exhausting labor, undernourishment, immoderate drinking, injury, irritations from foreign bodies (such as the lead gun-slug found lodged in the leg of a boy who went mad some years later), poisons, intestinal worms, harmful internal secretions, tumors, abscesses, and a number of diseases, such as apoplexy and epilepsy.

Insanity, Rush pointed out, could also be hereditary, or psychological in origin. Among the psychological causes, he listed driving ambition, great disappointment, terror, grief and other distresses, defamation, and ridicule. Another trigger could be a great loss — the loss of liberty, of beauty, of property. Men had gone insane from losses during the time of certificate speculation. Rush knew of an Indian who had lost his reason when he first saw his face in a mirror after being marked by smallpox, and of a man who had done the same after losing an eye in a tavern brawl. Great shock, then, could also cause insanity.

But are some people more prone to insanity than others? Rush believed so. The incidence of insanity among women, he said, was greater during pregnancy and childbirth. There was more insanity in the rich than in the poor, more among civilized people than among savages, more in cold, moist and cloudy climates than in dry, sunny climates.

JOHN RUSH's second question — Is it possible to cure insanity? — was even harder to answer than the first. Traditional treatment of the insane was as benighted, as barbarous, as the traditional explanations of why they were insane. If they were "possessed" by the devil or were being punished for their sins, the justice of treating them brutally was evident to every hag-ridden mind. In the Pennsylvania Hospital, they were confined in dark, unheated, poorly ventilated basement rooms, or cells, and treated with the same absence of charity as the inmates of fourteenth-century London's Bedlam, a "hospital" for "lunatics." Until the creation of the special insane ward, completed in 1796, Rush campaigned vainly against such heartless treatment. Besides being brutal, he said, it clearly did no good.

What would help? Nobody knew. It was only clear to Rush, the great experimental clinician, that if insanity was a disease, there might be a cure, and he began a search for it.

He was deep in clinical experiment even as early as 1787. In a letter to Dr. John Coakley Lettsom of London he said "The remedies on which I place my chief dependence are the warm and cold baths." He called the baths the "Indian Method." When a patient had been brought to a high pitch of excitement in a hot bath, he was plunged into a cold one. Rush kept a careful clinical record of the results.

He had run across the method during his study of Indian medical lore, on which he had lectured before the American Philosophical Society back in 1774. The "Oration" was published the same year. Evidently Thomas Jefferson, the all-curious, had read it or knew of it. At any rate, as President in 1803, when he received permission from Congress to have Lewis and Clark explore the great and unknown West, Jefferson asked Rush, the greatest doctor of them all, to draw up directions for preserving the health of the expedition, which would come in contact with Indian diseases. Rush complied, and took advantage of the opportunity to have Lewis and Clark find all possible answers to a long list of questions on Indian health.

Besides trying the Indian method, Rush attacked what he thought to be the purely physical causes of mental illness in a number of ways. He continued to use his purges and emetics to quiet the "morbid excitement" of the brain, but he soon gave up bloodletting in such cases. He also introduced two other methods which, though a bit rough and ready, were forerunners of modern therapies. One was the use of a "tranquilizer," a big wooden armchair with a head-sized hollow block hinged to the top of the chair-back. The patient was strapped in the chair, and the block swung down over his head and fixed. The purpose of the forerunner of the strait jacket was to immobilize the patient, thus preventing a rush of blood to the brain and diminishing the force and frequency of the pulse. The other soon-discarded device was a "gyrator," or turntable. While lying on it, his head toward the circumference, the patient was rapidly rotated. Its effect was opposite to that of the "tranquilizer," since the circular motion centrifuged blood to the brain.

LIKE all trial-and-error attempts to solve problems, Rush's attempts to strike at the physical causes of insanity were shots in the dark. Except for the "Indian Method," they were dreamed up, which does not make them any the less praiseworthy. The history of science is full of the happy results of trial and error.

Dr. Rush's Tranquilizing Chair

Two happy results of this kind, achieved by others, led Rush to what is known in modern psychiatry as "shock" treatment. A New York doctor, treating a woman for drug addiction, pulled a large snuffbox out of his pocket. The patient asked for a pinch of the snuff. When the doctor opened the box, a snake slithered onto her hand, up her arm and onto her shoulder. The shock of surprise and terrified repulsion, Rush had heard, broke the woman's drug habit.

Another and different trial was made by one of Rush's Philadelphia colleagues. He had a patient who refused to talk and spent day after day making drawings. On one visit the doctor found him sketching a flower. "A pretty cabbage," the doctor said. "You're a fool and a liar!" the patient yelled, breaking his long silence. "It's a flower!" The patient had been shocked into speech, and he did not relapse. Similar effects, Rush believed, might be obtained from other sudden excitements — loud and unusual sounds, great pain, sharp odors and, in 1812, he was the first to try electricity for this purpose. Electric shock is now widely used in psychiatry for seriously ill mental patients.

WHATEVER success Rush achieved in psychiatry by other means, his most significant contributions came from a kind heart and a solid common sense elevated by genius. It was his heart that revolted at the inhumane treatment of the insane, at their being gawked at as freaks and comic spectacles. It was his common sense that suggested the therapeutic value of changed surroundings, changed dress and changed company, of recreation, of occupational therapy. It was his genius that discovered the value of mental catharsis, that is, having patients write down their symptoms and "talk out" the misery of their troubled souls, as they do today to the psychoanalyst or psychiatrist.

Some of Rush's curative techniques were more than a century ahead of his time — his insistence on kindness and sympathy instead of ridicule and brutality, his use of physical and occupational therapy, of recreation, of mental catharsis. Also prophetic was his recognition of the role of the blood vessels in mental illness.

His five-volume *Medical Inquiries* was his major work in medicine. The fifth volume, on diseases of the mind, was the greatest of the five. It is now largely antiquated, but it remains one of the most important books on psychiatry ever written by an American. It has justly earned him the title of Father of American Psychiatry.

23. Summing Up

ON A SULTRY EVENING in the summer of 1800, Rush sat down to write his autobiography. At the top of a blank sheet of paper he wrote "Travels Through Life." It was time to sum up his travels. They had been full of snares and pitfalls. Perhaps the book would help his children and grandchildren avoid similar disasters. He picked up his pen and dipped it in the ink-pot.

> *"My dear children,*
> My life has been a variegated one. Under a conviction that I shall not live to give its details to the younger branches of my family, I have concluded to put upon paper a few incidents that may perhaps afford entertainment and instruction to them when I am no more. It is my wish that it may not

be read out of the circle of my family, and that it
may never be published."

That was a good enough beginning, but he hardly knew
how to continue. Dusk was falling, and his eyes were not as
sharp as they used to be. He lit the three candles on his
table. Their light somehow reminded him of a fall evening
in 1775 when he and an Englishman with "wonderful eyes"
had sat in the light of three candles and planned *Common
Sense* — a little book that was to work "a wonderful change
in the minds of men."

How should he go on? So much had happened before that
evening and after — so much in so short a time. Some had
been bad and some good — more good than bad. He himself had helped to win one revolution. Paine had helped to
win two, the French one as well as the American. And his
other battles — how many of them had there been! How
many blows he had taken and given! How many words had
he spoken and written! How many gross of candles had he
burned?

He had loved and lost two women and married a third —
the calm, capable, loving and beloved Julia. She had borne
him thirteen children. Nine of them had survived the hazards
of eighteenth-century childhood. John, the promising first-
born, had become troubled, changeable, and in ten more
years would be in the insane ward of the Pennsylvania Hospital. Richard, the second son, disregarding his father's
wishes, had gone into politics and had been disinherited for
his disobedience, though there is evidence that Rush took
pleasure in Richard's success. He would have taken more
pleasure, if he had been able to foresee that after his father's
death Richard would become Attorney General of the United States, acting Secretary of State under James Monroe, Minister to Great Britain, Secretary of the Treasury, Minister to

France, and running-mate to John Quincy Adams, in the latter's unsuccessful campaign for the presidency, in 1828.
James, his third son and his heir, was more satisfactory. He
became a doctor and, though Rush may not have approved
of it, married a girl with money and with social standing.
The younger boys did not particularly distinguish themselves. Neither did the three girls, who did the only thing
girls could do in those days — they found husbands.

"TRAVELS Through Life" went slowly. It was difficult to
choose the "entertainment and instruction" best suited for it.
Besides, even during his late years, the vigorous, hard-
working doctor was busy with many other things — with his
lectures at the Pennsylvania College, with editing, with formal writing. From 1801 to 1812, he produced a harvest of
new publications on medical, scientific and philosophical subjects. Four days before his death he wrote John Adams of two
more writing projects he was just about to begin.

The dynamo that was Benjamin Rush never stopped
whirring until it stopped for good. It generated more than
pamphlets and books. In his Plan for an Asylum for Drunk-
ards he continued his temperance crusade. He remained active in the various societies he had helped to found and even
founded a new one, the Philadelphia Bible Society.

He even found the time and charity of heart to attend William Shippen, Jr., in his last illness. Shippen turned out to be
forgiving, too. He "discovered after he was unable to speak,"
Rush reported, "that he carried no hostility out of the world
against me." Rush wished "Peace and joy to his departed
spirit." This was in 1808. Dr. Redman died the same year,
and Rush wrote and published a "tribute to the memory of
my dear and venerable master."

The next year Tom Paine died, and in 1809 Rush, with
John Adams, remembered that "He possessed a wonderful

talent of writing to the tempers and feelings of the public."
Paine, Rush also thought by then, was vain: "He once said
he was at a loss to know whether he was made for the times
or the times made for him." In the dusk of that long-ago
Christmas when old Tom's "wonderful talent of writing"
sent Washington's chilblained winter soldiers rushing into the
boats on the Delaware, it didn't make much difference whether Paine was made for the times or the times for Paine.

The dynamo whirred on. After 1800, only the three youngest children required the care and attention that, even in his
busiest years, he had lavished on his family. He should have
been able to ease off a little on his work, too, but to the last
Rush was always conscious of Time's winged chariot hurry-
ing on. His lung ailment and an occasional minor illness sometimes slowed him down, but not for long.

During the summers he did find relaxation and pleasure
at "the hut" on the little farm he had bought when it seemed
that he would have to resort to farming to feed his family.
One reason the place pleased him was that it gave Julia a
chance to enjoy her gardening. It was only two and a half
miles north of Philadelphia, close enough for Rush to com-
mute and take care of his practice, make his hospital rounds,
and attend to his duties at the Mint. He named the villa
"Sydenham" after Dr. Thomas Sydenham.

RUSH was built and rigged for storm. He made squadrons
of angry and bitter enemies. All strong, outspoken men do.
But he also made many devoted friends and admirers —
among the poor, among the Negroes, among the best men of
his time in America and abroad. The more than six hundred
and fifty of his letters — collected and admirably edited by
the historian, Dr. L. H. Butterfield, and published for the
American Philosophical Society by the Princeton University
Press (1950) — reveal the sharpness and pugnacity of spirit

that brought him enmity, abuse and slander. They also reveal the learning, the wit, the honesty, the amiability and the warmth that attracted Adams, Jefferson, Madison — and even, at the last, George Washington.

It has even been said that during the last thirteen years of his life Rush was deified. This is an exaggeration, though he did regain the public esteem he had lost during the worst of the fever epidemic years. It was almost inevitable that he should do so. Almost from his first day of practice and his first chemistry lecture, Dr. Rush had been a man to reckon with. Friend and foe alike, found it necessary, or advisable, to take account of what Rush was thinking, saying, writing and doing. Men ignored him or scoffed at him or attacked him at their peril, as William Cobbett discovered before he set sail.

His lines of force, powerful first and chiefly in Pennsylvania, extended in many directions and were felt in war and revolution, in state and national politics and legislation, in social welfare and the movement to abolish slavery, in education and religion, in medicine and science. They came to be felt throughout the nation he helped to found and in the citadels of culture and learning abroad. In 1808 two separate medals were struck in his honor at the United States Mint. Extremely rare, only two copies of one of the medals have been located. A measure of Europe's respect for him is the fact that when the great German explorer and scientist, Alexander von Humboldt, visited America in 1804, Benjamin Rush was one of the two men he most wanted to meet and talk with. The other man was Thomas Jefferson. And there are other measures. In 1805, the King of Prussia, impressed by Rush's account of the yellow fever epidemics, presented him with a coronation medal. In 1807, he received a gold medal from the Queen of Etruria and, in 1811, a diamond ring from the Czar of Russia.

Rush medal struck off by the U. S. Mint

His recognition abroad did not, of course, amount to deification, as Rush knew. Nor would the more belated recognition of him at home have astonished him. As a student of history, he knew that often prophets are honored everywhere but in their own country. He was doubtless hurt but not surprised, for example, when in 1812 his medical colleagues, except the younger doctors, greeted the publication of his great book on diseases of the mind with silence.

Among physicians of his own generation, especially in Philadelphia, the old animosities lingered on. Among younger men, so many of whom he had trained, he had an enormous following. Throughout the nation the Rush "system" of medicine had largely replaced Cullen's.

His name and medical reputation grew in luster with the years. His stature in the profession was recognized when a now-great Chicago medical college was named after him. A charter was granted to the Rush Medical College in 1837; in 1898, it became part of the University of Chicago as its Rush Graduate School of Medicine. Since 1941, it has been affiliated with the University of Illinois, one of whose Schools is in Chicago. As late as 1887 an eminent physician and writer, S. Weir Mitchell, acknowledged Rush as "the greatest physician this country has produced."

An almost identically phrased estimate appears in the report, published in 1890, of "A Rush Monument Committee of the American Medical Association . . . appointed in 1884." The report began: "Benjamin Rush to be commemorated as the greatest physician America has ever produced . . ." Unfortunately not enough funds were collected for the monument, but in 1960 the Association began a fresh attempt to "commemorate among many, Benjamin Rush . . . who shared honors with Benjamin Franklin as great Philadelphians of the 18th century."

In 1961 the Secretary of the Interior precipitated an uproar among physicians and sculptors by proposing that the statue of Rush in Washington, D.C., should be moved to his native state. Evidently the physicians and sculptors felt that moving the statue (maintained by the Navy Department on the grounds of The Bureau of Medicine and Surgery at 2300 E Street, N.W.) would impoverish the national capital. A century and a half after his death Benjamin Rush was again a storm center — this time with a happy difference.

The death of the illustrious subject of this uproar-with-a-difference came in 1813. At the end of a busy and, therefore, ordinary working day — April 14 — Dr. Rush sat down for dinner with his family. Suddenly he got up and went to his bedroom, complaining of a chill. During the night he developed a fever and severe pains in the side. The next day two colleagues from the medical college diagnosed the illness as typhus fever. Rush shook his head. "It's my lungs," he said. "It's pulmonary tuberculosis."

Five days later — April 19 — calm and clear of mind, he spoke his last words to Dr. James Rush, "the millionaire far up Chestnut Street," as his brother Samuel called him. "Be indulgent to the poor," said the doctor who loved Hermann Boerhaave, the old Dutch doctor who had said that "God is the paymaster of the poor."

The funeral was as simple as the man who was buried. A few close friends, a few representatives of scientific and philanthropic organizations saw the body lowered into a grave in Christ Church Burial Ground. He was joining good company there — six Signers of the Declaration of Independence, including Benjamin Franklin, and John and Susanna Rush. Julia, in her time, was laid beside him. On one side of them is the grave of John, their eldest, and on the other the grave of William, their youngest.

The much-reviled old fighter was dead. The rich and the poor, Negro and white, the exalted and the humble now

Statue of Benjamin Rush, Washington, D.C., Maintained by the U.S. Navy Department

acknowledged the great loss. John Adams, in a letter to Richard Rush, made the acknowledgment better than most:
"There is not another out of my own family ... in whom
my personal happiness can be so deeply affected ... in the
estimation of unprejudiced philosophy, he has done more
good in this world than Franklin and Washington." Thomas
Jefferson, in a letter to Adams, confirmed what the other
former President had said: "Another of our friends of sev-
enty-six is gone, my dear Sir, another of the co-signers of the
Independence of our country. And a better man than Rush
could not have left us, more benevolent, more learned, of
finer genius, or more honest."

*   *   *   *

IN his "accounts" — in *Travels Through Life* — of those who
signed the Declaration of Independence, the old doctor acknowledged himself in three words:

"BENJAMIN RUSH. He aimed well."

Index